£1

D1343863

THE SUMMER FRUITS
COOKBOOK

BY

CHARLOTTE POPESCU

CAVALIER COOKBOOKS
An imprint of Cavalier Paperbacks

© Charlotte Popescu 2002

Published by Cavalier Cookbooks 2002
Reprinted 2005, 2012

An imprint of Cavalier Paperbacks
Burnham House,
Upavon,
Wilts SN9 6DU

Cover illustration by Beverley Lees

ISBN 9781899470501

Printed and bound in Great Britain by Cox & Wyman,
Cardiff Road, Reading, Berks

CONTENTS

STRAWBERRIES

Strawberries were cultivated by the Romans in Britain but those that we enjoy today were developed from small strawberries in Virginia, USA and brought back to England by John Tradescant the Elder, the great seventeenth century gardener. They were crossed with larger yellow Chilean pine strawberries brought from South America to France by Frezier in the early 1700s. It wasn't until the early 1800s that large strawberries were being cultivated and sold in Britain. Popular varieties available today include Cambridge Favourite, Elsanta, Elvira, Girella and Hapil. Strawberries are an excellent source of vitamin C and B and contain potassium, iron and ellagic acid - a phytochemical which may fight against cancer. They are high in fibre but low in calories - 100g of strawberries = 27 calories.

Strawberries are delicious on their own or with cream, but they also work well served with balsamic vinegar and a little brown sugar or with chopped basil leaves and a little lemon juice. A sprinkling of freshly ground black pepper will heighten their flavour. It is best not to wash strawberries before using them and they do not freeze well but make excellent jam.

SAVOURY RECIPES

SWEET RECIPES

STRAWBERRY CHEESE DIP

Serves 4 – 6

100g, 4oz strawberries
75g, 3oz cream cheese
50g, 2oz blue cheese

Mash the strawberries. Add the cheeses and beat well together until the mixture is reasonably smooth. Chill and serve as a dip accompanied by pieces of cucumber, carrot, celery or crisps.

STRAWBERRY SOUP

Serves 4

240ml, 8fl oz dry white wine
75g, 3oz caster sugar
225g, 8oz strawberries, puréed
240ml, 8fl oz orange juice

Put the wine and sugar into a saucepan and boil for 5 minutes. Allow to cool. Stir into the puréed strawberries and then stir in the orange juice. Chill for several hours before serving.

STRAWBERRY, CUCUMBER AND CHICORY SALAD

Serves 6

225g, 8oz strawberries
half a cucumber
1 head of chicory

Dressing

6 tbsp olive oil
juice of a lemon
sprinkling of pepper
1 tsp chopped chives
1 tsp chopped parsley

Slice the strawberries and the cucumber and separate the chicory leaves. Arrange the chicory on a serving plate and scatter the strawberries and cucumber on top. Make the dressing by combining all the ingredients and pour it over the salad before serving.

AVOCADOS WITH STRAWBERRY DRESSING

This is a refreshing summer starter and very nutritious since avocados contain mono-unsaturated fats and are a good source of Vitamin E.

Serves 6

3 ripe avocados
lemon juice

Dressing

150ml, ¼pt olive oil
juice of half a lemon
150g, 6oz strawberries
salt and pepper

To make the dressing liquidise all the ingredients in a food processor until smooth. Cut the avocados in half, remove the stones, peel them and cut into neat slices. Brush with lemon juice to prevent them from going brown. Arrange on a serving plate and pour the strawberry dressing over them.

STRAWBERRY-FILLED PLAICE FILLETS

This is a light summer dish. You could serve it with rice and peas.

Serves 4

450g, 1lb strawberries
4 tbsp fresh chopped coriander
900g, 2lb plaice fillets
180ml, 6fl oz fish stock

Whiz 2 fillets of the plaice and the coriander in a food processor. Slice all the strawberries and stir three quarters of these in. Divide this filling between the remaining plaice fillets and roll them up. Place them in a large saucepan and pour over the stock. Cover and poach the fillets for 10 minutes. Remove the fish carefully and keep warm. Boil the stock to reduce by half, and add the remaining chopped strawberries. Pour the sauce over the plaice fillets and serve.

SALMON WITH STRAWBERRIES

A light, summery supper dish which you could serve
with new potatoes and mange tout.

Serves 2 – 3

225g, 8oz strawberries
3 spring onions, chopped
1 tbsp lemon juice
350g, 12oz salmon fillet, cut into strips
2 tbsp olive oil
100g, 4oz prawns
100g, 4oz mushrooms
2 tbsp chopped parsley

Mix together the strawberries, onions and lemon juice and
pour over the salmon. Leave to marinade for 30 minutes.
Then take the salmon strips out of the marinade and fry in
the olive oil for several minutes, turning them as they cook.
Add the prawns and mushrooms and stir in the marinade
with the strawberries. Simmer for a few more minutes to
allow the prawns to cook and then serve with the parsley
scattered on top.

STRAWBERRY AND LEMON CHEESECAKE

Serves 8

For the base

225g, 8oz digestive biscuits, crushed
100g, 4oz melted butter

For the topping

225g, 8oz cream cheese
3 tbsp caster sugar
1 tsp vanilla essence
juice and rind of 1 small lemon
3 eggs, separated
15g, ½oz gelatine and 2 tbsp warm water
300ml, ½pt double cream, whipped
225g, 8oz strawberries, sliced

Mix the crushed biscuits with the butter and use to line a greased, loose-bottomed 23cm (9in) cake tin. Bake for 10 minutes at gas mark 2, 140°C (300°F) and allow to cool. To make the filling beat the cream cheese, sugar and vanilla essence until smooth. Add the lemon juice, rind and the egg yolks and beat again. Dissolve the gelatine in the water and stir into the mixture. Beat the egg whites until stiff and fold them into the cream cheese mixture followed by the whipped cream. Spoon over the biscuit base and chill. Just before serving, remove the cheesecake from the tin and cover the top with strawberries.

STRAWBERRY SHORTBREAD WITH LEMON CURD

Serves 8

For the shortbread

150g, 6oz plain flour
50g, 2oz caster sugar
100g, 4oz butter

For the filling

3 tbsp lemon curd
150ml, ¼pt double cream

For the topping

350g, 12oz strawberries
icing sugar

Put the flour, butter and sugar in a food processor and process until the mixture binds together. Pat this mixture around the inside of a greased 23cm (9in) flan dish. Bake in a preheated oven at gas mark 4, 180°C (350°F) for 15 to 20 minutes or until just starting to brown at the edges. Allow to cool. Whisk together the lemon curd and cream and spread over the shortbread base. Cover with sliced strawberries, dust with icing sugar and serve at once cut into wedges.

STRAWBERRY AND RASPBERRY TIRAMISU

Serves 4 – 6

450g, 1lb strawberries
3 tbsp caster sugar
350g, 12oz raspberries
juice of half a lemon
3 tsp rosewater
1 packet of sponge fingers
150ml, ¼pt whipped cream

Slice the strawberries and sprinkle with 2 tablespoons of sugar. Purée the raspberries and mix with the lemon juice, rosewater and remaining sugar. Line the base of a serving bowl with sponge fingers, sugar side down. Cover with strawberries and pour over half the purée. Cover with more sponge fingers and another layer of strawberries. Pour the remaining raspberry purée over these. Chill in the fridge for at least a couple of hours. Cover with the whipped cream before serving.

STRAWBERRIES AND CREAM CHEESE PUDDING

Serves 4 – 6

450g, 1lb strawberries, sliced
75g, 3oz cream cheese
150ml, ¼pt single cream
1 tbsp caster sugar
1 tsp lemon juice
grated rind from half a lemon

Beat the cream cheese and cream together. Stir in the sugar, lemon rind and juice and mix in the strawberries. Serve at once.

STRAWBERRY AND MASCARPONE PUDDING

Serves 4 – 6

225g, 8oz mascarpone cheese
2 eggs, separated
2 tbsp brandy
125g, 5oz caster sugar
225g, 8oz strawberries, sliced

Beat together the mascarpone, egg yolks, brandy and caster sugar. Whisk the egg whites and fold them in. Spoon into a serving bowl and chill. Just before serving fold in the strawberries.

PEACHES WITH ELDERFLOWER-FLAVOURED STRAWBERRIES

Serves 6

6 ripe peaches, stoned and halved
juice of half a lemon
225g, 8oz strawberries
2 tbsp elderflower cordial
150g, 6oz mascarpone
2 tbsp golden caster sugar

Slice the strawberries and spoon the elderflower syrup over them. Allow them to marinade for 30 minutes, then gently fold them into the mascarpone. Brush the lemon juice over the halved peaches to prevent them discolouring. Transfer to a serving dish (one that can withstand a hot grill) and spoon the strawberry and mascarpone mixture into the holes left by the stones in the peaches. Sprinkle with the golden caster sugar. Place under a hot grill for a minute or until the mascarpone starts to melt. Serve immediately.

STRAWBERRY AND LEMON TIPSY TRIFLE

Serves 4 – 6

450g, 1lb strawberries, hulled and quartered
100g, 4oz macaroons, broken into pieces
90ml, 3fl oz sweet wine
3 tbsp set honey
1 tbsp brandy
2 tbsp lemon juice
150ml, ¼pt double cream
2 egg whites

Mix the strawberries with the macaroons and put in a large glass bowl. Pour 2 tablespoons of the wine over them. Mix together the remaining wine, honey, brandy and lemon juice. Whip the cream and gradually whisk into the wine mixture. Whisk the egg whites and fold into the cream mixture. Pour over the strawberries. Cover and chill for an hour before serving.

BUTTERSCOTCH PANCAKES WITH STRAWBERRIES

Serves 4

8 pancakes
75g, 3oz butter
3 tbsp golden syrup
150ml, ¼pt double cream, whipped
225g, 8oz strawberries

Melt the butter and golden syrup together. Bring to the boil and boil for 3 minutes. Chop the strawberries and fold gently into the cream. Fold the pancakes into quarters and arrange 2 on each plate. Drizzle over the sauce and top with a dollop of strawberries and cream.

STRAWBERRY CUSTARD

Children love this strawberry flavoured custard and it makes a few strawberries go a long way.

Serves 4 – 6

4 eggs, separated
210ml, 7fl oz hot milk
3 tbsp sugar
1 tsp vanilla essence
450ml, ¾pt double cream, whipped
350g, 12oz strawberries, puréed

Beat the egg yolks and sugar together until pale and thick. Stir in the hot milk and continue to stir over a gentle heat until the custard thickens. Stir in the vanilla essence and allow to cool. Beat the egg whites until stiff and fold them into the whipped cream, then fold in the custard and the strawberry purée. Serve immediately.

PEARS ARMANDINE

Pears and strawberries work well together and this is a light, healthy pudding. The strawberry purée drizzled over the pears adds a lovely colour to this dessert.

Serves 4

300ml, ½pt water
100g, 4oz sugar
1 tsp vanilla essence
4 pears, peeled, halved and cored
25g, 1oz flaked almonds
225g, 8oz strawberries

Boil the sugar and water for a few minutes. Add the vanilla and poach the pears in this syrup until they are just tender, turning them over once or twice. Put them in a serving dish and stick the almonds into the sides of the pears. Boil the syrup to reduce by half. Add the strawberries and boil for a few minutes, then sieve them and spoon over the pears. Chill and serve with cream.

STRAWBERRY CRÈME BRÛLÉE

Serves 4

150g, 6oz strawberries, sliced
2 egg yolks
1 tbsp caster sugar
300ml, ½pt double cream
3 tbsp demerara sugar

Divide the strawberries between 4 ramekin dishes. Beat the egg yolks in a bowl with the caster sugar until pale and thick. Heat the cream until almost boiling point and pour on to the egg yolks. Place the bowl over a pan of simmering water and cook, stirring until the mixture thickens. Allow to cool and then pour over the strawberries. Put in the fridge overnight or at least for a few hours. Then sprinkle the demerara sugar over the custard in each ramekin and place under a preheated grill until the sugar caramelises. Cool and chill before serving.

STRAWBERRY CRÈME CARAMEL

Serves 4

100g, 4oz granulated sugar
150ml, ¼pt water
600ml, 1pt milk
4 eggs, beaten
225g, 8oz strawberries, sliced

Topping

50g, 2oz golden granulated sugar

Put the sugar and water in a saucepan and heat gently until dissolved. Bring to the boil and boil rapidly until a golden caramel. This will take a few minutes but watch it carefully and remove it from the heat as soon as it turns brown. Warm the milk in a saucepan and pour onto the caramel. Be careful, the mixture will splutter. Stir until the caramel dissolves. Mix the beaten eggs into the caramel milk and pour into an ovenproof dish. Add the strawberries, cover with foil and place in a small roasting tin half filled with water. Bake in a preheated oven at gas mark 3, 160°C (325°F) until set. This will take about an hour. Remove from the oven and cool completely. Sprinkle with the golden granulated sugar and place under a hot grill until caramelised.

CHILLED STRAWBERRY SOUFFLÉ

A simple pudding ideal for weight watchers.

Serves 4

3 egg whites
225g, 8oz strawberries, puréed
50g, 2oz caster sugar
1 tbsp Kirsch

Whisk the egg whites until very stiff. Stir the sugar and Kirsch into the strawberry purée. Fold the egg whites into the strawberry mixture. Spoon into a greased soufflé mould and bake in a preheated oven at gas mark 4, 180°C (350°F) for about 4 minutes. Cool and chill. The soufflé should not drop when cold but may separate a little, in which case you can whisk it together again.

STRAWBERRY SNOW

Serves 4 - 6

450g, 1lb strawberries
75g, 3oz caster sugar
a few drops of vanilla essence
3 egg whites
150ml, ¼pt double cream, whipped

Purée and sieve the strawberries. Stir in the sugar and vanilla essence. Beat the egg whites until stiff and fold them into the purée along with the whipped cream.

STRAWBERRY AND KIWI FRUIT
LEMON SYLLABUB

Strawberries and kiwi fruit go rather well together. Kiwi fruit are an excellent source of vitamin C.

Serves 4 - 6

225g, 8oz strawberries
4 kiwi fruit, peeled
6 meringues, crushed
150ml, ¼pt double cream
2 tbsp crème fraîche
5 tbsp sweet white wine
3 tbsp lemon curd

Slice the kiwi fruit and arrange in the bottom of a serving dish. Chop the strawberries and mix gently with the crushed meringues. Scatter on top of the kiwi fruit. Whisk the cream, crème fraîche, wine and lemon curd together until thick. Spoon on top of the strawberries and chill before serving.

CARAMEL AND CRUSHED MERINGUES
WITH STRAWBERRIES

This pudding is for those with a sweet tooth.

Serves 6 – 8

1 large tin of condensed milk
600ml, 1pt double cream
8 meringues, crushed
350g, 12oz strawberries, sliced

Immerse the unopened tin of condensed milk in a saucepan of water and cook, gently simmering for at least an hour. Allow to cool a little before opening. The condensed milk will have cooked to a thick caramel. In a serving bowl spread a layer of cream, then a layer of meringue. Now spoon some of the condensed milk over the meringues. If the condensed milk has become very thick you can stir in a spoonful of milk to thin it a little. Next add a layer of strawberries. Repeat the layers, finishing with cream. Chill well before serving.

TRADITIONAL STRAWBERRY MOUSSE

Serves 4 – 6

15g, ½oz gelatine
2 tbsp water
3 eggs, separated
75g, 3oz caster sugar
225g, 8oz strawberries, puréed
150ml, ¼pt double cream, whipped

Dissolve the gelatine in the water over a very gentle heat. Whisk the egg yolks and sugar together until pale and thick. Whisk the egg whites until stiff. Fold the dissolved gelatine into the egg yolk mixture. Stir in the strawberry purée and cream. Lastly fold in the egg whites carefully and thoroughly. Spoon into a serving bowl and allow to set.

STRAWBERRY AND RASPBERRY
JELLIED MOUSSE

Serves 6 – 8

225g, 8oz strawberries
225g, 8oz raspberries
1 packet strawberry jelly
3 eggs, separated
50g, 2oz caster sugar

Sieve the fruit. Measure the purée and make up to 450ml (¾ pt) with water. Heat in a saucepan until it just reaches the boil. Then add the strawberry jelly and stir until melted. Put the egg yolks and sugar in a bowl and whisk until thick. Then gradually whisk the egg yolks into the jelly mixture. Leave to cool. Meanwhile whisk the egg whites and fold into the fruit mixture. Pour into a serving dish and chill before serving.

STRAWBERRY AND CASSIS SORBET

This is a sorbet strictly for adults as there is quite a lot of alcohol added. The alcohol keeps the sorbet softer than a normal water ice as the freezing point of alcohol is lower than that of water.

Serves 4

450g, 1lb strawberries
4 tbsp crème de cassis
400ml, 14fl oz dry white wine
2 tbsp caster sugar
2 egg whites

Purée the strawberries with the cassis, white wine and sugar until smooth. Pour into a freezer container and freeze for a couple of hours. Remove from the freezer and beat well. Whisk the egg whites and fold them into the semi-frozen mixture. Put back in the freezer and freeze until firm.

STRAWBERRY CREAM ICE

Serves 4 – 6

100g, 4oz caster sugar
150ml, ¼pt water
450g, 1lb strawberries, puréed
300ml, ½pt double cream
2 tsp vanilla essence

Dissolve the sugar in the water and simmer until syrupy which will take about 5 minutes. Allow to cool. Mix the strawberry purée with the sugar syrup. Whip the cream until it is thick and then fold into the strawberry mixture. Stir in the vanilla essence and pour the mixture into a freezer container. Freeze for at least 8 hours but remove from the freezer about 30 minutes before you want to serve it.

STRAWBERRY ICE CREAM

Serves 4

75g, 3oz sugar
4 egg yolks
150ml, ¼pt double cream, whipped
350g, 12oz strawberries, puréed and sieved
1 tbsp orange juice

Dissolve the sugar in 4 tablespoons of water. Bring to the boil and boil vigorously for a couple of minutes. Meanwhile whisk the egg yolks until pale and thick and gradually whisk in the sugar syrup. Whisk until cool and thick. Fold in the cream. Stir the orange juice into the strawberry purée and fold it into the egg yolk mixture. Pour into a freezer container and freeze until firm.

STRAWBERRY AND ELDERFLOWER JAM

Makes about 2.7kg (6lb)

1.4kg, 3lb strawberries, hulled
1.4kg, 3lb granulated sugar
juice of 1 lemon
50g, 2oz redcurrants
2 handfuls of elderflowers

Put the strawberries, sugar, lemon juice and redcurrants in a preserving pan and add the elderflowers, stripping them from their stems. Cover the pan and leave in a warm place for 2 or 3 hours. Then place the pan over a gentle heat and stir every so often until the sugar dissolves. Raise the heat and boil rapidly. After about 15 minutes test for a set. If a little jam placed on a saucer wrinkles when you push it then the jam is set. If not, boil for a little longer and test again. Turn off the heat and leave in the pan for 20 minutes before pouring into warmed jars and sealing.

RASPBERRIES

Wild raspberries have been around since prehistoric times but were not cultivated until the Middle Ages. There are now many varieties that you can grow yourself and there are some excellent autumn ripening varieties including Autumn Bliss and Autumn Gold which produces yellow raspberries. Raspberries are a good source of Vitamin C, potassium, niacin, and riboflavin and are one of the best fresh fruit sources of fibre. Low in calories - 100g = 25 calories - and more versatile than strawberries, raspberries freeze very well.

SAVOURY RECIPES

SWEET RECIPES

RASPBERRY SOUP

Serves 4

450g, 1lb raspberries
2 tbsp honey
5 tbsp red wine
150ml, ¼pt carton of soured cream

Sieve the raspberries. Mix the honey, 2 tablespoons of the red wine and 2 of water and stir over a low heat until dissolved. Leave to cool and then add the raspberry purée, half of the soured cream, the rest of the wine and 210ml (7 fl oz) of water. Stir well and chill. Serve with a spoonful of soured cream topping each portion.

PORK AND RASPBERRY STIR-FRY

Serves 3 – 4

450g, 1lb pork tenderloin, cut into strips
2 tbsp olive oil
2.5cm, 1in fresh root ginger, sliced
2 carrots, peeled and sliced into sticks
handful of curly kale, shredded
225g, 8oz raspberries
1 tbsp dark soya sauce

Heat the oil in a wok, add the ginger and stir-fry for half a minute. Add the pork strips and fry for 2 minutes, then add the carrots and cook for a couple more minutes. Toss in the kale and raspberries and allow to heat through. Pour over the soya sauce. Serve with noodles.

DUCK WITH RASPBERRIES

This is an excellent healthy and nutritious main course. Serve with new potatoes and broccoli or French beans.

Serves 4

4 duck breasts, skin removed
2 tbsp raspberry vinegar
2 tbsp brandy
1 tbsp clear honey
oil for brushing

Sauce

225g, 8oz raspberries
300ml, ½pt rosé wine
2 tsp cornflour blended with a little water

Score the duck breasts and pound with a meat mallet until they are less than 2cms (¾in) thick. Mix together the vinegar, brandy and honey and spoon over the duck. Allow to marinade in this mixture for about an hour. Place the duck breasts on a grill and reserve the marinade. Season and brush with oil. Cook for 10 minutes on each side. To make the sauce put the reserved marinade in a saucepan and add 150g (6oz) of the raspberries and the wine. Bring to the boil and simmer for 5 minutes. Strain the sauce through a sieve. Return to the pan and stir in the cornflour paste, which will thicken the sauce. Heat through, adding the extra raspberries and pour over the duck breasts before serving.

APPLE AND RASPBERRY SPONGE

A delicious family pudding.

Serves 4 - 6

25g, 1oz butter
450g, 1lb Cox's apples, peeled, cored and chopped
450g, 1lb raspberries
1 tbsp lemon juice
75g, 3oz demerara sugar

Sponge

100g, 4oz margarine
100g, 4oz caster sugar
100g, 4oz self-raising flour
2 medium eggs
1 tbsp milk
1 tsp grated lemon zest

Melt the butter in a large saucepan and add the chopped apples, raspberries, lemon juice and sugar. Gently heat to dissolve the sugar and cook for 5 minutes. Tip the whole mixture into an ovenproof dish. To make the sponge combine all the ingredients in a food processor or cream together the margarine and sugar and add the eggs gradually with the flour, milk and lemon zest. Spread the sponge mixture over the apples and raspberries. Cook in a preheated oven at gas mark 4, 180°C (350°F) for 30 minutes. Serve hot with cream.

RASPBERRY AND BRAMLEY CRUMBLE

Serves 6

450g, 1lb cooking apples, peeled, cored and sliced
225g, 8oz raspberries
100g, 4oz caster sugar
2 tbsp water

Crumble

50g, 2oz plain flour
50g, 2oz porridge oats
50g, 2oz ground almonds
75g, 3oz butter
50g, 2oz brown sugar

Put the sliced apples in a pie dish with the raspberries, caster sugar and water. Put the flour and oats in a bowl with the ground almonds. Add the butter and rub with the fingertips until the mixture resembles breadcrumbs. Stir in the brown sugar. Pile the crumble mixture on top of the fruit. Bake in a preheated oven at gas mark 4, 180°C (350°F) for 30 to 40 minutes or until the crumble topping is golden brown.

RASPBERRY SHORTBREAD CRUMBLE

Serves 4 – 6

450g, 1lb raspberries
1 tbsp caster sugar

Crumble

150g, 6oz plain flour
1 tsp baking powder
½ tsp ground ginger
50g, 2oz butter
100g, 4oz light muscovado sugar

Put the raspberries in a shallow ovenproof dish and sprinkle with the caster sugar. Sieve the flour, baking powder and ginger together. Rub the butter into the flour and stir in the brown sugar. Spread this mixture over the raspberries and smooth it out evenly. Bake in a preheated oven at gas mark 4, 180°C (350°F) for about 25 minutes. Serve hot with cream.

ROSE-FLAVOURED RASPBERRY STREUSEL TART

Serves 8

For the sweet pastry

100g, 4oz plain flour
50g, 2oz butter
25g, 1oz icing sugar
1 egg yolk

350g, 12oz raspberries
50g, 2oz caster sugar
1 tbsp rosewater

For the crumble

100g, 4oz plain flour
25g, 1oz cornflour
50g, 2oz butter
25g, 1oz golden granulated sugar

To make the pastry process the flour, butter and icing sugar. Add the egg yolk and enough water to bind to a dough. Wrap in cling film and chill for 30 minutes. Roll out the pastry and use to line a 20cm (8in) flan tin. Bake blind in the oven at gas mark 5, 190°C (375°F) for 15 minutes. Meanwhile add the sugar and rosewater to the raspberries and leave them to infuse. To make the crumble process the flour, cornflour and butter until the mixture resembles breadcrumbs. Stir in the sugar. Spread the raspberries over the pastry and scatter the crumble topping over them. Bake in the oven for a further 30 minutes. Serve hot with cream.

RASPBERRY AND HAZELNUT CAKE

This cake is unusual in that it is made with egg whites rather than whole eggs - you could use the egg yolks to make an ice cream or a crème brulée.

Serves 8

100g, 4oz butter
125g, 5oz caster sugar
75g, 3oz plain flour
1 tsp baking powder
100g, 4oz ground hazelnuts
5 egg whites
150ml, ¼pt double cream
225g, 8oz raspberries

Cream together the butter and sugar. Sift the flour with the baking powder, stir in the hazelnuts and beat into the butter and sugar. Whisk the egg whites and fold them into the mixture a third at a time. Place in a greased 20cm (8in) cake tin and cook in a preheated oven at gas mark 4, 180°C (350°F) for about 25 to 30 minutes. Allow to cool in the tin, then turn out and cut in half. Whip the cream and fold into the raspberries. Sandwich the 2 halves of cake together with the cream and raspberries. Dust with icing sugar before serving.

PEAR AND RASPBERRY PAVLOVA

Serves 6 – 8

For the pavlova

4 egg whites
225g, 8oz caster sugar
½ tbsp cornflour, sifted
1 tsp white wine vinegar
1 tsp vanilla essence

For the topping

150ml, ¼pt whipping cream
150ml, ¼pt soured cream
225g, 8oz pears, peeled, cored and sliced
225g, 8oz raspberries
50g, 2oz sugar

To make the pavlova, beat the egg whites until stiff. Gradually beat in the sugar, a little at a time. Sprinkle the cornflour, vinegar and vanilla over the mixture and fold in carefully. Make a circle with the meringue mixture on a large greased baking sheet. Bake for an hour at gas mark 1, 120°C (275°F). The pavlova should be crisp on the outside with a soft marshmallow centre. Whip the cream with the soured cream. Spread this over the meringue. Cook the raspberries with the sugar over a gentle heat until the juices run. Add the pears and cook for a couple more minutes. Carefully pour the pear slices and raspberries over the cream and serve at once.

RASPBERRY AND PEAR COMPOTE WITH ELDERFLOWER CREAM

Serves 4

25g, 1oz sugar
6 heads of fresh elderflowers
150ml, ¼pt double cream, whipped
450g, 1lb pears, peeled and chopped
450g, 1lb raspberries
300ml, ½pt apple juice
1 cinnamon stick
2 strips of lemon rind

First make the elderflower cream. Put the sugar and 150ml (¼pt) of water in a saucepan and heat gently to dissolve the sugar. Then boil rapidly to reduce the liquid by half. Remove from the heat and add the elderflowers. Leave to infuse for at least an hour. Then strain the syrup and fold in the whipped cream. Put the pears in a saucepan with the apple juice, cinnamon stick and lemon rind and simmer for 10 minutes until the pears have softened. Add the raspberries and simmer for another 5 minutes. Remove the cinnamon stick and lemon rind and serve warm with the elderflower cream.

RASPBERRY AND ALMOND PUDDING

Serves 4

350g, 12oz raspberries
4 egg yolks and 2 egg whites
100g, 4oz sugar
100g, 4oz ground almonds
50g, 2oz melted butter

Put the raspberries in a greased, shallow ovenproof dish. Beat the egg yolks until thick and pale, then beat in the sugar and almonds and stir in the melted butter. Whip the egg whites until stiff and fold into the egg yolk mixture. Pour on top of the raspberries and bake in a preheated oven at gas mark 4, 180°C (350°F) for about 30 minutes until risen and golden brown. The pudding may sink a little as it cools. Serve with cream.

RASPBERRY TOPPED SHORTCAKE

Serves 4 - 6

150g, 6oz plain flour
100g, 4oz butter
50g, 2oz caster sugar
1 egg yolk
450g, 1lb raspberries

Glaze

4 tbsp redcurrant jelly
1 tbsp water

Rub the butter into the flour until the mixture resembles breadcrumbs. Add the sugar and egg yolk and bind the mixture together. Roll out and press into a 23cm (9in) greased flan dish. Prick all over with a fork and bake in a preheated oven at gas mark 4, 180°C (350°F) for 25 minutes. Allow to cool. Arrange the raspberries over this shortcake base. Blend together the redcurrant jelly and water and melt in a pan over a gentle heat. Spoon over the fruit. Serve cut into slices with cream.

RASPBERRY TARTLETS

Serves 4 – 5

Sweet pastry

225g, 8oz plain flour
125g, 5oz butter
3 tbsp icing sugar
1 egg yolk

Filling

100g, 4oz cream cheese
150ml, ¼pt double cream
1 tbsp caster sugar
1 egg white
350g, 12oz raspberries
icing sugar

Put all the ingredients for the pastry into a food processor and process until the mixture binds together. Wrap in cling film and chill for 30 minutes. Then roll out into rounds and fit into the base of 4 or 5 greased tartlet tins. Bake blind in a preheated oven at gas mark 4, 180°C (350°F) for 10 to 15 minutes and allow to cool. Beat the cream cheese and cream together. Mix in the caster sugar. Whisk the egg white and fold into the cream cheese mixture. Spoon onto the pastry bases and top with the raspberries. Dust with icing sugar and serve.

LIGHT LEMON PUDDING CAKE

Serves 8

100g, 4oz self-raising flour
125g, 5oz caster sugar
4 tbsp sunflower oil
3 eggs, separated
grated rind of 1 lemon
½ tsp cream of tartar

Syrup

Juice of 1 lemon
2 tbsp water
100g, 4oz sugar

150ml, ¼pt double cream
150ml, ¼pt Greek yoghurt
225g, 8oz raspberries

Sift together the flour and sugar in a large bowl. Make a
well in the centre and add the oil, egg yolks, lemon rind
and 5 tablespoons of water. Beat the batter until smooth.
Add the cream of tartar to the egg whites and whisk until
stiff. Fold the egg whites into the batter and pour into a
deep ring mould. Bake at gas mark 3, 160°C (325°F) for
an hour. Leave in the tin to cool. To make the syrup heat
the lemon juice, water and sugar gently in a small saucepan until the sugar has dissolved. Then bring to the boil
and boil for 2 minutes. Turn the pudding out of the ring
mould and pour the syrup over the sponge. Beat together
the double cream and Greek yoghurt and spoon into the
middle of the cake. Pile the raspberries on top of the cream
and sprinkle with icing sugar if liked.

LEMON AND RASPBERRY TRIFLE

Serves 6

225g, 8oz sponge cake (see page 35)
rind and juice of 2 lemons
3 eggs, separated
1 large tin of condensed milk
350g, 12oz raspberries
150ml, ¼pt double cream, whipped

Crumble the sponges into a serving bowl. Beat the egg yolks with the condensed milk and the lemon rind and juice until thick. Moisten the sponge with a little of the mixture. Whisk the egg whites and fold them into the remaining lemon mixture. Pour over the sponge. Top with the raspberries and finish with a layer of the whipped cream.

RASPBERRY SOUFFLÉ OMELETTE

Serves 2

3 eggs, separated
50g, 2oz caster sugar
rind and juice of 1 lemon
15g, ½oz butter
100g, 4oz raspberries

Beat the egg yolks with the sugar, rind and lemon juice. Whisk the egg whites in a separate bowl until stiff. Fold them into the egg yolk mixture. Heat the butter in a large frying pan and pour the omelette mixture into the pan. Cook for a couple of minutes and then sprinkle the raspberries over the omelette. Fold over and cook for a couple more minutes. Serve at once.

CREAM-FILLED BRIOCHES WITH RASPBERRIES

Serves 6

6 brioche rolls
225g, 8oz mascarpone
1 tbsp icing sugar
1 tbsp blackcurrant juice
15g, ½oz butter
225g, 8oz raspberries
2 tbsp caster sugar

Slice the tops off the brioche rolls, scoop out the centres and discard. Mix together the mascarpone, icing sugar and blackcurrant juice and spoon into the rolls. Melt the butter in a frying pan and stir in the caster sugar. Add the raspberries and cook until they start to release their juices. Then spoon equal amounts on top of the cream and blackcurrant mixture. Dust with icing sugar and serve.

STUFFED PEACHES WITH RASPBERRIES

Serves 8

8 peaches
8 macaroons, crushed
2 egg yolks
2 tbsp Marsala
50g, 2oz chopped almonds
100g, 4oz sugar
grated rind of half a lemon
sprinkling of white wine
knob of butter
225g, 8oz raspberries

Cut the peaches in half and remove the stones. Hollow out some of the flesh and reserve. Grease an ovenproof dish and place the peach halves on it. Mix the peach flesh with the crushed macaroons and add the egg yolks, Marsala, almonds, sugar and grated lemon rind. Mix well and stuff a little mixture into each peach half. Scatter the raspberries over and around the peaches. Dot with butter and sprinkle with white wine. Cook in a preheated oven at gas mark 5, 190°C (375°F) for about 20 minutes. Serve with crème fraîche.

RASPBERRY FRITTERS WITH LEMON SAUCE

Serves 6 – 8

Lemon sauce

rind and juice of 1 lemon
25g, 1oz butter
50g, 2oz sugar
2 eggs, beaten

Batter

250ml, 9fl oz water
50g, 2oz butter
25g, 1oz caster sugar
100g, 4oz plain flour
25g, 1oz ground almonds
3 eggs
100g, 4oz raspberries

To make the lemon sauce boil the lemon rind in 150ml (¼pt) of water for 5 minutes. Then add the sugar, butter, lemon juice and beaten eggs. Stir carefully over a gentle heat until the mixture thickens. Strain and keep warm to serve with the fritters. To make the batter put the water, butter and sugar into a saucepan and bring to the boil. Stir in the flour and beat until the mixture comes away from the sides of the pan. Beat in the ground almonds and eggs, one at a time. Fold in the raspberries. Heat the oil in a deep frying pan and drop small spoonfuls of the batter into the oil. Deep fry the fritters in batches for a couple of minutes until golden. Drain and keep warm while you cook all the fritters. Serve dusted with icing sugar and accompanied by the sauce.

RASPBERRY RICE CREAM

This is a fruity version of a rice pudding but is served cold. My children love it.

Serves 4 – 6

75g, 3oz short grain rice
600ml, 1pt milk
100g, 4oz caster sugar
2 eggs, separated
225g, 8oz raspberries

Put the rice in a saucepan with the milk and half the sugar. Bring to the boil, then lower the heat and simmer gently until all the milk is absorbed. Remove from the heat and mix in the egg yolks. Cover with cling film and leave the mixture to cool. Whisk the egg whites and whisk in the rest of the sugar. Fold into the rice and lastly mix in the raspberries.

RASPBERRY CRÈME BRÛLÉE

Serves 4

225g, 8oz raspberries
2 tbsp brandy
4 egg yolks
300ml, ½pt double cream
125g, 5oz golden caster sugar

Pour the brandy over the raspberries and allow to soak in for at least 30 minutes. Bring the cream to the boil with 25g (1oz) of the caster sugar. Allow to cool. Beat the egg yolks with the cream and place in a small bowl over a pan of simmering water. Cook slowly until the mixture thickens. Put the raspberries into 4 buttered ramekin dishes and cover with the egg and cream mixture. Leave to chill overnight. The next day sprinkle each one with a tablespoon of golden caster sugar and put under the grill until the sugar caramelises. Leave to cool and the top will become crisp.

RASPBERRY AND REDCURRANT MOUSSE

Serves 4 – 6

225g, 8oz raspberries
225g, 8oz redcurrants
150g, 6oz sugar
2 egg whites

Sieve the raspberries and redcurrants to remove all pips. Add the sugar. Whisk the egg whites until stiff and fold into the purée. In a saucepan over a low heat whisk the mixture for about 3 minutes until the mixture thickens and starts to rise. Pour into glasses or a serving bowl and leave to cool before serving. If left for a while some of the juice will separate and sink to the bottom but can be whipped up again before serving.

RASPBERRY SORBET

Serves 4

225g, 8oz raspberries, puréed and sieved
juice of half a lemon
75g, 3oz caster sugar
2 egg whites

Add the lemon juice and sugar to the puréed raspberries and mix well. Pour into a freezer container and freeze until the slushy stage. Beat well and return to the freezer. After another hour, beat again. Whisk the egg whites and fold them into the half frozen mixture. Return to the freezer and freeze until you are ready to serve it. Sorbets are best eaten within a day or two of being frozen.

RASPBERRY ICE CREAM

This is a delicious ice cream. You don't need an ice cream maker and you don't need to beat the mixture once you have put it in the freezer.

Serves 6 – 8

450g, 1lb raspberries, puréed and sieved
2 tbsp icing sugar
squeeze of lemon juice
120ml, 4fl oz water
75g, 3oz sugar
3 egg yolks
300ml, ½pt double cream

Add the icing sugar and lemon juice to the sieved raspberries. Dissolve the sugar in the water and then bring to the boil and keep it boiling for a couple of minutes. Meanwhile whisk the egg yolks until pale and thick and then slowly whisk in the sugar syrup in a steady stream. Continue to whisk the mixture as it cools. Fold the egg yolk mixture into the raspberry purée. Whip the cream and fold that in too. Stir until the mixture is smooth. Pour into a freezer container and freeze until firm.

RASPBERRY AND WATERMELON CREAM ICE

Serves 4 – 6

4 tbsp clear honey
juice of ½ lemon
150ml, ¼pt whipping cream
150ml, ¼pt Greek yoghurt
225g, 8oz raspberries
1 watermelon

Whisk the honey and lemon juice. Whip the cream. Fold the honey and lemon into the cream and yoghurt. Fold in the raspberries. Cut the watermelon in half. Remove the seeds and purée the flesh. Add this to the cream mixture and stir everything together until well incorporated. Pour into a freezer container and freeze until firm.

RASPBERRY WATER ICE

Serves 6

225g, 8oz sugar
150ml, ¼pt water
350g, 12oz raspberries
juice of 2 lemons
juice of 2 oranges

Put the sugar and water in a small saucepan and dissolve the sugar over a low heat. Bring slowly to the boil and boil fast for a minute. Allow to cool. Sieve the raspberries and add the lemon and orange juice. Stir in the cooled sugar syrup. Pour into a freezer container and freeze for about 4 hours. Transfer to the fridge for 30 minutes before serving. Turn the mixture over a few times with a metal spoon and then put into chilled glasses or into a serving bowl.

RASPBERRY SURPRISE MERINGUES
WITH RASPBERRY SAUCE

These could be served at tea-time on their own or as a
pudding with the raspberry sauce.

Makes approximately 20 meringues

4 egg whites
225g, 8oz golden caster sugar
20 large raspberries

For the sauce

225g, 8oz raspberries
25g, 1oz icing sugar

Whip up the egg whites until very stiff. Whisk in half the
sugar and fold in the rest carefully until well incorporated.
Use a dessertspoon and put spoonfuls of this meringue
mixture onto greased baking sheets. Press 1 raspberry into
each meringue and carefully cover them so that they are
enclosed. Bake in the oven at gas mark ½, 120°C (250°F)
for about 2 hours. To make the sauce purée the raspberries
with the icing sugar and sieve to remove the pips. Stack
the meringues up on a plate or serve with the sauce and
some whipped cream if feeling indulgent.

RASPBERRY AND LIME DRIZZLED CAKE

Lime and raspberries go rather well together in this cake.

Serves 8

150g, 6oz butter
150g, 6oz golden caster sugar
3 large eggs
175g, 7oz self-raising flour
25g, 1oz flaked almonds
grated rind and juice of 1 lime
225g, 8oz raspberries

For the syrup

Juice of 2 limes
Grated peel of 1 lime
100g, 4oz granulated sugar

Cream together the butter and sugar. Gradually beat in the eggs and mix in the flour, flaked almonds and grated rind. Lastly stir in the lime juice. Fold in three quarters of the raspberries. Grease and line a 20cm (8in) deep cake tin and spoon the mixture into it. Smooth the surface and scatter the remaining raspberries on top. They will sink into the cake as it rises. Bake in a preheated oven at gas mark 4, 180°C (350°F) for about 40 minutes or until a skewer pushed into the centre comes out clean. To make the syrup put the lime juice, peel and sugar in a small saucepan and heat gently, allowing most of the sugar to dissolve. As soon as the cake comes out of the oven, prick all over with the skewer and drizzle the lime syrup over the cake. Allow to cool before turning out.

RASPBERRY CAKE WITH
RASPBERRY BUTTER CREAM

Serves 6 – 8

3 eggs, separated
100g, 4oz caster sugar
1 tbsp lemon juice
grated rind of 1 lemon
75g, 3oz self-raising flour, sifted

For the butter cream

75g, 3oz butter
100g, 4oz icing sugar
100g, 4oz raspberries

For the topping

150ml, ¼pt double cream, whipped
100g, 4oz raspberries

Whisk the egg yolks with the sugar until pale and thick. Fold in the lemon juice, rind and flour. Whisk the egg whites until stiff and fold them in. Spoon the sponge mixture into 2 greased 17.5cm (7in) cake tins and cook in a preheated oven at gas mark 4, 180°C (350°F) for 15 minutes. Cool before turning out. To make the raspberry butter cream, beat the butter and icing sugar together and beat in the raspberries. Then sieve the mixture to remove the pips. Spread the butter cream over one half of the cake and top with the other half. Top with more raspberries folded into the cream.

RASPBERRY AND REDCURRANT JELLY

Makes about 2.5kg (5lb)

1.35kg, 3lb raspberries
450g, 1lb redcurrants
300ml, ½pt water
2kg, 4¼lb preserving sugar

Place the raspberries, redcurrants and water in a large saucepan. Stir over a low heat until the juices begin to run, then simmer until very soft. Sieve the raspberries and redcurrants to remove pips. Put the purée back in the pan and add the sugar. Stir over a low heat until the sugar has dissolved. Then bring to the boil and boil rapidly for 3 or 4 minutes. Test for a setting. When a soft set has been reached, allow to cool and then pour into warmed jars and seal.

EASY RASPBERRY JAM

Makes about 3.5kg (8lb)

2kg, 4¼lb raspberries
2kg, 4¼lb caster sugar

Warm the sugar in the oven or in a microwave. Gently crush the fruit, transfer to a large saucepan and heat gently until simmering. Stir in the warm sugar and when it has dissolved bring to boiling point. Then remove from the heat and stir in any skin that has formed. Spoon into warmed jars and seal.

RASPBERRY VINEGAR

Makes about 900ml (1½pt)

1kg, 2lb 2oz raspberries
600ml, 1pt distilled white malt vinegar
granulated sugar

Crush the raspberries against the side of a bowl with a wooden spoon. Pour over the vinegar, cover with a thick cloth and leave for a couple of days. Strain through a muslin bag. Add 450g (1lb) of sugar for every 600ml (1pt) of juice and heat gently in a large saucepan until the sugar has dissolved. Bring to the boil and boil rapidly for 10 minutes, skimming off any scum that appears. Pour into hot sterilised bottles and cork.

TAYBERRIES

Tayberries are a cross between a raspberry and a blackberry. They were first cultivated in Scotland when raspberries were crossed with American blackberries. Dr Derek Jennings bred the first tayberries at the Scottish Crop Research Institute and the tayberry is named after the River Tay. Tayberries are thought to be the most successful hybrid berry.

SWEET RECIPES

TAYBERRY AND AMARETTO TRIFLE

Serves 4

2 egg yolks
75g, 3oz caster sugar
225g, 8oz mascarpone
2 tbsp Amaretto liqueur
1 egg white
450g, 1lb tayberries
150g, 6oz macaroons, crushed

Whisk the egg yolks and sugar together. Gradually whisk in the mascarpone and Amaretto liqueur. Whisk the egg white and fold into the mascarpone mixture. Make layers in a serving dish of tayberries, then some of the mascarpone mixture, then some of the crushed macaroons. Repeat the layers ending with the macaroons.

TAYBERRY AND CHOCOLATE TARTLETS

Tayberries and chocolate go rather well together.

Makes 4 – 5 tartlets

For the pastry

225g, 8oz plain flour
125g, 5oz butter
3 tbsp icing sugar
1 egg yolk

Topping

100g, 4oz milk chocolate
225g, 8oz fromage frais
150g, 6oz Greek yoghurt
350g, 12oz tayberries
icing sugar

Put all the ingredients for the pastry into a food processor and process until the mixture binds together. Wrap in cling film and chill for 30 minutes. Then roll out into rounds and fit into the base of 4 or 5 greased tartlet tins. Bake the pastry blind in a preheated oven at gas mark 4, 180°C (350°F) for 10 to 15 minutes and then cool. Divide the tayberries between the tartlets. To make the topping beat together the fromage frais and yoghurt. Melt the chocolate and quickly stir into the fromage frais mixture. It will start setting immediately. Spoon over the tayberries. Dust with icing sugar and serve.

TAYBERRY AND NECTARINE
TOFFEE PUDDINGS

These are delicious little puddings made in ramekins
suitable for a family supper or for a supper party. You
could use raspberries and peaches instead of the
tayberries and nectarines.

Serves 4

4 nectarines, stoned
100g, 4oz tayberries
50g, 2oz butter
50g, 2oz caster sugar
2 tbsp double cream
50g, 2oz brown breadcrumbs
25g, 1oz brown sugar
15g, ½oz plain flour
½ tsp mixed spice

Cut the nectarines into small chunks. Place the butter, sugar
and cream in a small saucepan and heat gently until the
butter is melted and the sugar dissolved. Spoon half this
mixture into the base of 4 ramekin dishes and top with the
chopped nectarines and some tayberries. Mix together the
breadcrumbs, brown sugar, flour and mixed spice. Spoon
some over the fruit. Lay the rest of the nectarines and
tayberries over the breadcrumb mixture and drizzle over
the rest of the buttery mixture. Bake in a preheated oven
at gas mark 4, 180°C (350°F) for 30 minutes. Cool slightly
before serving with whipped cream.

TAYBERRY AND REDCURRANT CRUMBLE

Serves 4 – 6

225g, 8oz tayberries
225g, 8oz redcurrants
75g, 3oz caster sugar
1 tbsp semolina
100g, 4oz plain flour
75g, 3oz butter
50g, 2oz caster sugar

Place the tayberries and redcurrants in an ovenproof dish and sprinkle over the sugar and semolina. To make the crumble rub the butter into the flour and stir in the sugar. Spread over the fruit mixture and pack down lightly. Bake in a preheated oven at gas mark 5, 190°C (375°F) for about 30 minutes. Serve hot with cream.

TAYBERRY SOUFFLÉ PUDDING

Serves 4 – 6

450g, 1lb tayberries
100g, 4oz caster sugar
25g, 1oz butter, warmed
100g, 4oz white breadcrumbs
3 eggs, beaten

Warm the tayberries with the sugar over a low heat until the juices begin to run, sieve them and mix in the butter and breadcrumbs. Stir in the eggs and pour into a greased 1 litre (2 pint) baking dish. Bake in a preheated oven at gas mark 4, 180°C (350°F) for 30 minutes. Leave to cool slightly, dust with icing sugar if liked and serve with cream.

TAYBERRY AND LEMON CREAM CRUNCH

Serves 6

1 packet ginger biscuits
75g, 3oz butter, melted
300ml, ½pt crème fraîche
225g, 8oz lemon curd
675g, 1½lb tayberries
icing sugar for sprinkling

Crush the biscuits and mix with the melted butter. Mix together the crème fraîche and lemon curd. Make a layer of biscuit crumbs at the bottom of a glass bowl. Follow this with a layer of lemon cream and then a layer of tayberries. Continue the layers finishing with a layer of tayberries. Dust with icing sugar before serving.

TAYBERRY YOGHURT ICE

Serves 4

450g, 1lb tayberries, puréed and sieved
150ml, ¼pt plain yoghurt
100g, 4oz icing sugar
2 tbsp lemon juice
150ml, ¼pt double cream
2 egg whites

Mix the tayberries, yoghurt, icing sugar and lemon juice together until smooth. Whip the cream and fold into the tayberry mixture. Pour into a container and freeze until just becoming firm. Whisk the egg whites until stiff and fold them into the half frozen ice cream. Return to the freezer and freeze until firm.

LOGANBERRIES

Similar to the tayberry, the loganberry is also a cross between a raspberry and a blackberry. The loganberry was named after JH Logan of California who first grew them in 1881. Loganberries are not as sweet as tayberries and need sweetening if eaten fresh. They are good cooked and make excellent jam.

SWEET RECIPES

SPICED LOGANBERRY SPONGE PUDDING

Serves 6 – 8

450g, 1lb loganberries
4 tbsp golden syrup

For the sponge

100g, 4oz margarine
100g, 4oz caster sugar
2 eggs
100g, 4oz self-raising flour
½ tsp mixed spice
2 tbsp milk

Put the loganberries in a greased ovenproof dish and spoon over the golden syrup. Cream together the margarine and sugar, beat in the eggs and fold in the flour, mixed spice and milk. Spread over the top of the loganberries and cook in a preheated oven at gas mark 4, 180°C (350°F) for about 40 minutes. Serve hot with cream or crème fraîche.

LOGANBERRY AND LEMON BAVAROIS

Serves 6 - 8

Sponge base

2 eggs, beaten
50g, 2oz caster sugar
50g, 2oz plain flour, sifted

Bavarois

450ml, ¾pt milk
grated peel and juice of 2 lemons
1 tsp vanilla essence
5 egg yolks
125g, 5oz caster sugar
4 tsp gelatine
300ml, ½pt whipping cream, whipped
225g, 8oz loganberries

Make the sponge by whisking together the eggs and sugar and then folding in the flour. Pour into a 20cm (8in) greased, deep, springform cake tin and bake in a preheated oven at gas mark 4, 180°C (350°F) for 20 minutes. To make the bavarois, put the milk, lemon peel and vanilla essence into a saucepan and slowly bring to the boil. Beat the egg yolks and sugar together until thick and then whisk in the hot milk. Cook stirring constantly until thick. Warm the gelatine in 4 tablespoons of water until dissolved, mix in a little custard and then stir in the rest. Stir in the lemon juice and fold in the cream. The mixture will gradually set. Scatter the loganberries over the sponge base and then pour the custard on top. Chill before turning out.

LOGANBERRY AND APPLE CAKE WITH CLOVES

Serves 8

150g, 6oz self-raising flour
2 tsp ground cloves
100g, 4oz margarine
75g, 3oz caster sugar
225g, 8oz loganberries
375g, 12oz apples, cored, peeled and grated
3 eggs, beaten

Sift the flour with the ground cloves and rub in the margarine. Stir in the sugar, loganberries and apples. Add the eggs and stir everything together until well mixed. Pour the mixture into a greased 20cm (8in) cake tin and cook in a preheated oven at gas mark 4, 180°C (350°F) for about 50 minutes, until cooked through but still slightly moist in the centre. Turn out and serve warm or cold with cream.

LOGANBERRY AND PEAR
UPSIDE DOWN PUDDING

Serves 4 – 6

100g, 4oz golden syrup
grated rind of 1 lemon
100g, 4oz loganberries
3 pears, peeled, cored and sliced

For the cake

100g, 4oz butter
100g, 4oz brown sugar
100g, 4oz self-raising flour
2 eggs
2 tbsp milk

Spoon the golden syrup into the base of a lightly greased 20cm (8in) deep cake tin. Arrange the loganberries and pear slices over the golden syrup and scatter the lemon rind on as well. To make the sponge beat together all the ingredients and spoon over the fruit. Bake in a preheated oven at gas mark 4, 180°C (350°F) for 35 minutes and cool in the tin a little before turning out. Serve warm with cream.

LOGANBERRY MOUSSE

Serves 4 - 6

450g, 1lb loganberries
juice of 1 lemon
3 eggs, separated
125g, 5oz caster sugar
25g, 1oz gelatine
300ml, ½pt double cream, whipped

Put the loganberries in a saucepan with the lemon juice and heat gently until the juices begin to run. Purée and sieve them and leave to cool. Put 3 tablespoons of water in a small saucepan and sprinkle on the gelatine. Heat gently until the gelatine is dissolved. Whisk the egg yolks and gradually add the caster sugar, whisking until they are pale and thick. Stir in the loganberry purée and the dissolved gelatine. Fold in the whipped cream. Lastly whisk the egg whites until stiff and fold them in. Pour into a serving bowl and chill to set.

LOGANBERRY SNOW

There is no cream in this recipe and you can use a low
fat cream cheese if you are watching your weight.

Serves 4

350g, 12oz loganberries
1 tbsp rosewater
50g, 2oz sugar
150g, 6oz cream cheese
2 egg whites
50g, 2oz icing sugar

Cook the loganberries in a little water until they soften.
Purée and sieve them. Add the rosewater. Cool and then
freeze the puréed loganberries until the slushy stage. Beat
the sugar and cream cheese together and beat into the half
frozen loganberries. Freeze until just firm. When you are
ready to serve the pudding, whisk the egg whites with the
icing sugar and fold into the loganberry mixture to give a
swirled effect.

LOGANBERRY WATER ICE

Serves 4 – 6

450g, 1lb loganberries, sieved
100g, 4oz sugar
150ml, ¼pt water
3 lemon-scented geranium leaves

Make a syrup by dissolving the sugar in the water over a gentle heat and then add the geranium leaves and boil for 5 minutes. Strain to remove the geranium leaves and when cool mix into the loganberry purée, pour into a freezer container and freeze until firm.

LOGANBERRY MERINGUE
ICE CREAM PUDDING

Serves 8

600ml, 1pt double cream, whipped
50g, 2oz light muscovado sugar
2 tbsp cocoa, sifted
8 meringues, crushed
450g, 1lb loganberries

Stir the sugar and cocoa into the cream along with the crushed meringues. Cut up the loganberries and fold them in. Spoon the mixture into a freezer container and smooth the top. Cover and freeze for about 4 hours. An hour before serving, transfer to the fridge. Turn out of the freezer container and dust with icing sugar before serving.

LOGANBERRY MUFFINS

Makes 12

225g, 8oz plain flour
2 tsp baking powder
50g, 2oz caster sugar
1 egg, beaten
300ml, ½pt milk
50g, 2oz butter
100g, 4oz loganberries

Sift the flour and baking powder and add the caster sugar. Make a well in the centre and add the milk and egg. Mix together and then gradually beat in the butter. Fold in the loganberries. Divide the mixture between 12 greased muffin cases. Bake in a preheated oven at gas mark 6, 200°C (400°F) for 20 minutes.

LOGANBERRY JAM

Makes about 2.7kg (6lb)

2kg, 4¼lb loganberries, under-ripe and unwashed
2kg, 4¼lb sugar

Put the loganberries in a large saucepan, and gently heat them until the juices start to run. Now leave to cook slowly for 30 minutes. Meanwhile warm the sugar; this could be done in the microwave. Add the hot sugar to the loganberries and cook for another 15 minutes, or until all the sugar has dissolved. Then boil the jam on the highest heat for 10 minutes. Spoon a little onto a plate and push with your finger to see if it crinkles and is jelly-like. If not boil for a few more minutes and test again until the jam has set. Leave the jam for 15 minutes and add a little knob of butter to get rid of any scum that has formed. Then pour into warmed jars and seal.

BLACKCURRANTS

Blackcurrants grow wild all over Europe. The English started to cultivate them in the 1600s. They are very rich in vitamin C and contain the anti-cancer carotenoid lutein. They are also a good source of vitamin E and provide moderate amounts of calcium and magnesium. Low in calories - 100g of blackcurrants = 28 calories - blackcurrants are high in pectin and therefore suitable for jams and jellies. Too acidic to eat on their own, they are wonderful cooked with sugar, puréed and added to yoghurt or cream or other fruits. They are easy to grow and you can expect each bush to produce a good yield of fruit each summer.

SAVOURY RECIPES

SWEET RECIPES

BEEF AND BLACKCURRANT KEBABS

Serves 4

225g, 8oz lean minced beef
1 tbsp fresh coriander, chopped
salt and pepper
75g, 3oz blackcurrants, sieved
12 small onions, blanched for 2 minutes in boiling water
12 button mushrooms
12 cherry tomatoes

Mix together the minced beef, coriander, blackcurrant purée and a sprinkling of salt and pepper. Divide the mixture into 12 and roll into balls. Chill for at least 30 minutes. Then thread onto four skewers alternating the meat balls with tomatoes, mushrooms and onion pieces. Grill for 10 minutes, turning every so often. Serve with rice sprinkled with soya sauce.

GRIDDLED DUCK BREASTS WITH BLACKCURRANT SALSA

New potatoes and a green vegetable such as mange
tout would go well with this dish.

Serves 4

4 duck breasts

Salsa

225g, 8oz blackcurrants
4 tsp sugar
1 tbsp white wine vinegar
350g, 12oz cherry tomatoes, chopped
a handful of mint
4 spring onions

To make the salsa heat the blackcurrants in a small saucepan with the sugar and vinegar and cook for a few minutes
until the juices run. Leave to cool a little and then mix in
the tomatoes, mint and onions. Set aside while you pre-
pare the duck breasts. Score the skin on each one through
to the flesh (this allows the fat to be released and the skin
to go crispy). Heat a griddle pan until hot. Add the duck
breasts and cook for 10 minutes on the skin side and about
6 minutes on the other side. Cut the duck breasts into slices
and serve with the salsa.

BLACKCURRANT AND APPLE WITH HAZELNUT CRUMBLE

Blackcurrants and apples go rather well together and this is a delicious crumble.

Serves 4 – 6

225g, 8oz blackcurrants
75g, 3oz granulated sugar
450g, 1lb cooking apples, peeled and cored
1 tbsp brown sugar

For the crumble

125g, 5oz plain flour
25g, 1oz hazelnuts
100g, 4oz butter
50g, 2oz caster sugar

Heat the blackcurrants with the sugar for a few minutes until the juices run and sieve them to produce a smooth purée. Slice the apples into an ovenproof dish and pour the purée on top. Sprinkle with the brown sugar. To make the crumble, put all the ingredients in a food processor and process until the mixture is crumbly. Spread over the top of the apple slices and blackcurrant purée. Bake in a preheated oven at gas mark 5, 190°C (375°F) for 30 minutes. Serve hot with cream.

LEMON AND BLACKCURRANT
SURPRISE PUDDING

The addition of blackcurrants underneath the sponge
topping makes a nice surprise.

Serves 6 - 8

450g, 1lb blackcurrants
75g, 3oz brown sugar
75g, 3oz butter
225g, 8oz caster sugar
grated rind of 2 lemons
6 eggs, separated
50g, 2oz flour
300ml, ½pt milk

Put the blackcurrants in the bottom of an ovenproof dish
and sprinkle with the brown sugar. Cream the butter and
caster sugar together and mix in the grated lemon rind.
Beat in the egg yolks one at a time and add the flour and
milk. Whisk the egg whites until stiff and fold them in
making sure everything is well mixed. Pour on top of the
blackcurrants. Stand the dish in a roasting tin half filled
with water. Put into a preheated oven at gas mark 4, 180°C
(350°F) and cook for about 40 minutes. Serve warm with
cream.

BLACKCURRANT AND TREACLE PUDDING

This is a simple steamed pudding but great for a family
supper.

Serves 4 – 6

2 tbsp golden syrup
100g, 4oz blackcurrant purée
100g, 4oz self-raising flour
100g, 4oz caster sugar
2 eggs
100g, 4oz margarine

Spread the golden syrup over the bottom and sides of a 1.2
litre (2 pint) pudding basin. Pour the purée into the pudding basin as well. Put the flour, sugar, eggs and margarine
into a food processor and process until well mixed. Spoon
on top of the blackcurrant purée. Cover the pudding basin
loosely with greaseproof paper and secure with a rubber
band. Put the pudding basin in a steamer and cook for about
an hour. Turn out onto a serving dish and serve with plenty
of cream.

BLACKCURRANT AND HAZELNUT TART

Blackcurrants and hazelnuts go rather well together.

Serves 6

For the pastry

75g, 3oz butter
25g, 1oz margarine
125g, 5oz plain flour
25g, 1oz ground hazelnuts
25g, 1oz caster sugar

For the filling

50g, 2oz semolina
75g, 3oz caster sugar
450g, 1lb blackcurrants

Rub the fats into the flour in a large bowl. Stir in the hazelnuts and sugar. Mix to a dough with a little cold water. Roll out and use to line a greased 20cm (8in) flan dish. Stir together the semolina and caster sugar and spread half over the base of the flan. Then scatter the blackcurrants on top of the sugar and semolina and sprinkle the rest of the sugary mixture over the top. Arrange any left over pastry in strips across the top of the tart and brush with a little beaten egg if liked. Bake in a preheated oven at gas mark 6, 200°C (400°F) for 30 minutes. Serve hot or cold.

CARAMELIZED BLACKCURRANT TART

Serves 6 - 8

For the almond pastry

150g, 6oz plain flour
75g, 3oz ground almonds
100g, 4oz butter
75g, 3oz caster sugar
1 egg, beaten

350g, 12oz blackcurrants
50g, 2oz granulated sugar
½ tsp cinnamon
2 eggs plus 2 egg yolks
300ml, ½pt whipping cream
3 tbsp cassis
2 tbsp golden caster sugar

Mix together the flour and almonds. Add the butter, sugar and egg to the dry ingredients and work together with your fingertips until you have a soft dough. Knead until smooth, wrap in cling film and chill for 30 minutes. Roll out and use to line the base of a greased 20cm (8in) flan dish. Bake blind in the oven at gas mark 4, 180°C (350°F) for 15 minutes. Allow to cool. Cook the blackcurrants with the sugar, 2 tablespoons of water and the cinnamon for a few minutes until softened. Cool before spreading over the pastry. Whisk together the eggs, cream, cassis and a tablespoon of the caster sugar. Pour over the blackcurrants. Return to the oven for about 20 minutes until the custard is just set. Sprinkle with the rest of the caster sugar and caramelise under a hot grill, being careful not to burn the pastry.

PEAR AND BLACKCURRANT STREUSEL PIE

Blackcurrants and pears go rather well together and, contrary to what you might expect, the blackcurrants don't swamp the pears.

Serves 6 - 8

225g, 8oz shortcrust pastry

Filling

450g, 1lb pears, peeled and sliced
225g, 8oz blackcurrants
100g, 4oz caster sugar
75g, 3oz plain flour
25g, 1oz ground almonds
50g, 2oz butter
150ml, ¼pt double cream
50g, 2oz caster sugar
pinch of nutmeg

Roll out the pastry and use to line a greased 20cm (8in) round deep pie dish. Make the filling by mixing the sliced pears and blackcurrants together. Stir together the flour and sugar and rub in the butter using your fingertips. Sprinkle half this mixture over the pastry. Spread the pears and blackcurrants evenly over this. Pour over the cream. Spoon over the remaining rubbed-in mixture and sprinkle with the caster sugar and nutmeg. Bake in a preheated oven at gas mark 6, 200°C (400°F) for 40 minutes. Allow to cool slightly before serving.

BLACKCURRANT CLAFOUTIS

Serves 6

450g, 1lb blackcurrants
100g, 4oz plain flour
2 eggs
300ml, ½pt milk
25g, 1oz butter
75g, 3oz caster sugar

Sift the flour into a bowl and make a well in the centre. Crack one whole egg and one egg yolk into the well and add half the milk. Stir the liquid in with a wooden spoon, gradually drawing in the flour. Beat to a smooth batter and stir in the remaining milk. Whisk the egg white and fold it in. Butter a baking dish and put it in the oven at gas mark 6, 200°C (400°F) to warm up. Remove and scatter the blackcurrants over the base. Immediately pour over the batter and return to the oven for 30 minutes or until risen and golden brown. Sprinkle the caster sugar all over the top of the batter and serve with cream.

BLACKCURRANT SPONGE PUDDING

Serves 6 - 8

225g, 8oz blackcurrants
50g, 2oz granulated sugar

For the sponge

100g, 4oz self-raising flour
1 tsp baking powder
2 eggs
100g, 4oz caster sugar
100g, 4oz margarine

Spread the blackcurrants and sugar over the base of a greased ovenproof dish. Put the flour, baking powder, eggs, sugar and margarine in a food processor and process until you have a smooth mixture. Spread over the top of the blackcurrants and cook in a preheated oven at gas mark 4, 180°C (350°F) for 35 to 40 minutes. Serve hot with cream or ice cream.

BLACKCURRANT AND CHOCOLATE TRIFLE

Serves 6 – 8

For the sponge

100g, 4oz margarine
100g, 4oz caster sugar
100g, 4oz self-raising flour
2 eggs

350g, 12oz blackcurrants
100g, 4oz sugar
½tsp cinnamon
100g, 4oz plain chocolate
2 eggs
15g, ½oz butter
150ml, ¼pt double cream, whipped

To make the sponge, cream together the margarine and sugar. Gradually add the eggs and flour. Beat together well and spoon into a greased 20cm (8in) cake tin. Bake in the oven at gas mark 4, 180°C (350°F) for about 25 minutes. Turn out, break into pieces and use to cover the base of a serving dish. Cook the blackcurrants with the sugar, a couple of tablespoons of water and the cinnamon until softened. Pour over the sponge. Melt the chocolate with the butter over a gentle heat. Beat the egg yolks into the chocolate mixture. Whisk the egg whites and fold these into the chocolate mixture. Spread over the blackcurrants. Cover with the whipped double cream. Chill until ready to serve.

BLACKCURRANT AND RICOTTA DESSERT

Serves 4

225g, 8oz blackcurrants
50g, 2oz caster sugar
1 tsp cornflour
100g, 4oz ricotta cheese
150ml, ¼pt Greek yoghurt
2 tbsp honey

Cook the blackcurrants in a saucepan with the sugar and a tablespoon of water for about 10 minutes. Mix the cornflour to a paste with a few drops of water and blend into the blackcurrant mixture. Cook for a couple more minutes. Beat together the ricotta cheese, Greek yoghurt and honey and place in a serving bowl. Pour the blackcurrant mixture over the top and swirl it around with a knife to give a marbled effect. Serve at once.

BLACKCURRANT SOUFFLÉ

Serves 6 – 8

450g, 1lb blackcurrants, puréed and sieved
4 eggs, separated
100g, 4oz caster sugar
juice of half a lemon
15g, ½oz gelatine
150ml, ¼pt cream, whipped

Put the sugar, egg yolks, blackcurrant purée and lemon juice in a mixing bowl and beat until thick. Melt the gelatine in a little hot water and pour onto the egg and fruit purée, whisking all the time. Fold in the cream and lastly whisk the egg whites and fold them in as well. Chill until set.

BLACKCURRANT CREAM

A quick, easy and delicious blackcurrant pudding.

Serves 4 - 6

450g, 1lb blackcurrants
100g, 4oz caster sugar
300ml, ½pt double cream, whipped
2 tbsp Greek yoghurt

Put the blackcurrants and sugar in a saucepan, cover and bring to the boil. Then allow to simmer for a few minutes. Remove from the heat and sieve them. Fold the cream and yoghurt into the blackcurrant purée and serve.

BLACKCURRANT AND PORT JELLY

Serves 5 – 6

450g, 1lb blackcurrants
225g, 8oz sugar
150ml, ¼pt ruby port
50g, 2oz gelatine

Put the blackcurrants and sugar into a saucepan and cover with water. Boil until soft and sieve them to remove all the pips. Sprinkle the gelatine over 150ml (¼pt) of water and heat gently until it dissolves. Pour onto the blackcurrant purée and stir. Add the port. Transfer to a jelly mould and chill to set. When ready to serve invert the jelly onto a plate and serve with cream.

MINT AND BLACKCURRANT MOUSSE

The flavour of mint goes rather well with blackcurrants.

Serves 8

450g, 1lb blackcurrants
150g, 6oz caster sugar
2 handfuls of applemint
3 eggs, separated
juice of 1 lemon
15g, ½oz gelatine
300ml, ½pt double cream, whipped

Put the blackcurrants in a saucepan and cook with 50g (2oz) of the sugar over a gentle heat until the juices begin to run and they are soft. Then purée the blackcurrants with the mint leaves and sieve to remove the pips. Dissolve the gelatine in the lemon juice over a gentle heat. Whisk the egg yolks with the remaining sugar until thick and creamy and whisk the gelatine mixture into the yolks. Fold in the blackcurrant purée. Leave until beginning to set and then gently fold in the cream. Lastly whisk the egg whites until stiff and fold them in. Pour into a serving bowl and allow to set in the fridge.

BLACKCURRANT KISSEL

This pudding is quite runny and has the consistency of thick soup. It goes well with a lemon or vanilla ice cream.

Serves 4 - 6

450g, 1lb blackcurrants
3 tbsp clear honey
juice of 1 lemon
pinch of nutmeg
1 – 2 tbsp caster sugar
25g, 1oz wholemeal flour

Put the blackcurrants, honey and lemon juice into a saucepan with enough cold water just to cover the fruit. Heat gently and simmer until the fruit is soft. Sieve the fruit and add a pinch of nutmeg. At this stage taste the purée. If it is too tart add the caster sugar. Put the flour into a bowl and stir in some of the blackcurrant mixture to make a paste. Mix this paste into the rest of the purée and stir over a low heat until thickened. Cool before serving.

BLACKCURRANT, YOGHURT AND NUT CREAM

Serves 4 – 6

225g, 8oz blackcurrants
100g, 4oz caster sugar
25g, 1oz medium oatmeal, toasted
25g, 1oz chopped almonds, toasted
1 tbsp lemon juice
25g, 1oz muscovado sugar
150ml, ¼pt Greek yoghurt
150ml, ¼pt double cream, whipped

Cook the blackcurrants with the sugar over a low heat until the juices run. Cool slightly and sieve the blackcurrants to produce a purée. Mix the oatmeal and almonds into the Greek yoghurt and add the muscovado and lemon juice. Fold in the double cream. Lastly swirl in the blackcurrant purée to give a marbled effect.

BLACKCURRANT LEAF CREAM

Serves 4

225g, 8oz granulated sugar
a handful of blackcurrant leaves
1 egg white
juice of half a lemon
100ml, 3½fl oz double cream, whipped

Dissolve the sugar in 150ml (¼pt) water over a low heat. Put in the leaves and boil for 15 minutes. Beat the egg white until stiff, then strain the boiling syrup onto the egg white and continue beating until the mixture is very thick. Stir in the lemon juice and then the cream. Divide between individual glasses or spoon into a glass bowl. This mixture can also be frozen.

BLACKCURRANT AND LIME SORBET

Serves 6 – 8

300ml, ½pt water
150g, 6oz granulated sugar
juice of 1 lime
450g, 1lb blackcurrants
2 egg whites

Put the water and sugar in a saucepan and heat gently until the sugar has dissolved. Bring to the boil and boil for 5 minutes until syrupy. Remove from the heat, stir in the lime juice and leave to cool. Meanwhile put the blackcurrants in a saucepan and heat gently until the juices start to run which should be after about 5 minutes. Sieve the blackcurrants and stir the blackcurrant purée into the cooled syrup. Freeze for an hour and then beat thoroughly. Whisk the egg whites until stiff and fold these into the blackcurrant mixture. Freeze until firm.

BLACKCURRANT LEAF WATER ICE

This is a useful way of using blackcurrant leaves and makes a very refreshing water ice.

Serves 6 – 8

Juice and rind from 3 lemons
4 handfuls of blackcurrant leaves
175g, 7oz sugar
900ml, 1½pt water
1 egg white

Dissolve the sugar in the lemon juice and the water. Bring to the boil and boil for 4 minutes. Add the blackcurrant leaves and lemon rind and leave to infuse for 40 minutes. Strain and press as much liquid as you can from the blackcurrant leaves. Pour into a freezer container and freeze until the slushy stage. Then beat the mixture, whisk the egg white and add to the half frozen mixture. Freeze until firm.

BLACKCURRANT ICE CREAM

Serves 6 – 8

450g, 1lb blackcurrants
2 tbsp caster sugar
squeeze of lemon juice
75g, 3oz granulated sugar
120ml, 4fl oz water
3 egg yolks
300ml, ½pt double cream, whipped

Soften the blackcurrants with a little water over a gentle
heat until the juices run and then sieve them. Add 2 tablespoons of sugar to sweeten them and a squeeze of lemon
juice. Dissolve the granulated sugar in the water over a
gentle heat. Then bring to the boil and boil rapidly for several minutes. Meanwhile whisk the egg yolks until pale
and thick and gradually whisk in the sugar syrup. Stir in
the blackcurrant purée and then fold in the whipped cream.
Spoon into a freezer container and freeze until firm.

APPLE AND BLACKCURRANT
ICE CREAM

The apples blend well with the blackcurrants and make
this ice cream less strong than a pure blackcurrant one.
My children love it.

Serves 8

225g, 8oz cooking apples, peeled, cored and chopped
225g, 8oz blackcurrants
2 tbsp granulated sugar
4 tbsp water
4 eggs, separated
100g, 4oz caster sugar
300ml, ½pt cream, whipped

Combine the apples, blackcurrants, granulated sugar and
water and simmer for 15 minutes. Sieve the fruit to remove the blackcurrant pips. Whisk the egg whites and
whisk in the caster sugar. Whisk the egg yolks until thick
and creamy. Fold the fruit purée into the whipped cream
and fold in the egg yolks. Lastly fold in the egg whites.
Pour into a freezer container and freeze until firm.

BLACKCURRANT JELLY

Blackcurrants are naturally rich in pectin and so do not need a preserving sugar but need a higher proportion of sugar and more water can be used than with other fruits to produce a higher yield.

Makes about 2.7kg (6lb)

2kg, 4¼lb blackcurrants
1.8 litre, 3pt water
1.35kg, 3lb sugar

Put the blackcurrants, including any stalks, in a large saucepan with the water, cover and simmer gently until soft. Strain through a jelly bag. Return the juice to the pan and add the sugar. Stir over a gentle heat until the sugar has dissolved then boil until setting point is reached. This may take about 15 to 20 minutes. Pour into warmed jars. Seal straightaway and store.

CRÈME DE CASSIS
(BLACKCURRANT LIQUEUR)

Makes about 900ml (1½pt)

450g, 1lb blackcurrants
1 stick of cinnamon
2 cloves
6 blackcurrant leaves
600ml, 1pt brandy
350g, 12oz sugar

Put the blackcurrants in a bowl and mash them up. Transfer them to a large sealable jar and add the spices, blackcurrant leaves and sugar. Pour the brandy over the blackcurrants and leave in a warm place for at least a month. Strain, squeezing out as much juice as you can. Pour into sterilised bottles and cork.

REDCURRANTS

Although redcurrants are closely related to blackcurrants and often combined with them in summer puddings they are different in several ways. They are planted, pruned and cared for like gooseberries and grown on old wood, unlike blackcurrants. They have a much softer skin and can be eaten raw. Like blackcurrants they are also a good source of Vitamin C. Whitecurrants are similar to redcurrants but lack the pigment.

SAVOURY RECIPES

SWEET RECIPES

BARBECUED CHICKEN WITH
REDCURRANT MARINADE

Serves 4

75g, 3oz redcurrant jelly (see page 114)
4 tbsp lemon juice
4 tbsp oil
4 tbsp chicken stock
½ tsp dry mustard
salt and pepper
½ tsp Worcestershire sauce
4 chicken pieces

Melt the jelly in a saucepan. Stir in the lemon juice, oil, stock, mustard, Worcestershire sauce and salt and pepper to taste. Arrange the chicken in a shallow dish and pour over the jelly mixture. Cover and leave to marinade overnight or for at least 4 hours. Take the chicken out of the marinade and barbecue until cooked through, basting with the redcurrant sauce and turning frequently.

SAUTÉED VEAL WITH REDCURRANTS AND CREAM

This dish is good served with new potatoes and mange tout.

Serves 4

450g, 1lb veal, cut into small pieces
1 tbsp plain flour
salt and pepper
25g, 1oz butter
4 spring onions, sliced
150ml, ¼pt dry white wine
2 tbsp cassis
150ml, ¼pt single cream
100g, 4oz redcurrants

Season the pieces of veal with salt and pepper and dust with flour. Melt the butter in a large frying pan and fry the spring onions. Add the veal and fry for a few minutes, turning once. Add the white wine and cassis and bubble for a minute. Stir in the cream and redcurrants and heat through. Spoon onto a dish and serve.

EASY REDCURRANT AND APPLE STRUDEL

Serves 4 - 6

225g, 8oz puff pastry
4 large cooking apples, peeled, cored and sliced
2 tbsp soft brown sugar
1 tsp vanilla essence
100g, 4oz butter
4 tbsp breadcrumbs
2 tbsp redcurrant jelly (see page 114)
50g, 2oz chopped almonds
icing sugar

Sprinkle the apple slices with brown sugar and the vanilla essence. Roll the pastry as thinly as possible on a well floured tea-towel into a rectangle. Melt 50g (2oz) of the butter in a pan and fry the breadcrumbs until golden. Melt the rest of the butter and spread over the pastry. Sprinkle the breadcrumbs over the pastry, spreading the apples over the top. Dot with the redcurrant jelly and the almonds. Fold in the edges of the pastry and roll up like a Swiss roll. Place the strudel on a buttered baking tin and brush again with melted butter. Bake in a preheated oven at gas mark 4, 180°C (350°F) for about 45 minutes, brushing with butter every so often. Dust with icing sugar and serve with cream.

DANISH REDCURRANT CAKE

Serves 4

225g, 8oz redcurrants
225g, 8oz brown breadcrumbs
75g, 3oz butter
4 tbsp brown sugar
150ml, ¼pt double cream, whipped

Melt the butter in a frying pan and add the breadcrumbs and 2 tablespoons of the sugar. Fry, stirring until the breadcrumbs are crisp. Place half the crumbs in the bottom of a small, round ovenproof dish about 15cm (6in) in diameter. Place the redcurrants on top and sprinkle with sugar. Finish with the remaining crumbs. Bake in a preheated oven at gas mark 4, 180°C (350°F) for about 20 minutes. Leave to cool in the tin and then cover with the whipped cream.

APPLE AND REDCURRANT CRUMBLE

Serves 4 – 6

450g, 1lb cooking apples, peeled and sliced
100g, 4oz redcurrants
2 tbsp caster sugar

For the crumble

75g, 3oz butter
75g, 3oz brown sugar
100g, 4oz porridge oats
1 tbsp sunflower seeds

Place the sliced apple and redcurrants together in a saucepan and allow to simmer for a few minutes to soften the fruit. Transfer the fruit to a baking dish and sprinkle on the sugar. To make the crumble melt the butter and stir in the brown sugar and oats. Spread this flapjack-type mixture over the fruit and sprinkle with sunflower seeds. Bake in the oven at gas mark 4, 180°C (350°F) for about 25 minutes. Serve hot with cream.

REDCURRANT AND PEAR COBBLER

Serves 4

½ tsp cinnamon
¼ tsp nutmeg
1 tsp cornflour
150ml, ¼pt water
225g, 8oz redcurrants
100g, 4oz sugar
2 large pears, peeled and sliced
150g, 6oz wholemeal flour
1 tsp baking powder
40g, 1½oz melted butter
1 egg
150ml, ¼pt soured cream

Mix the spices and cornflour and gradually add the water to make a smooth paste. Put the redcurrants and 50g (2oz) of the sugar in a saucepan, add the liquid paste and bring gradually to the boil and simmer for 3 minutes. Put the pears in a baking dish and pour over the redcurrant mixture. Meanwhile mix the flour, the rest of the sugar and the baking powder in a bowl. Add the melted butter, egg and soured cream and mix together. Drop spoonfuls of this mixture over the pears and redcurrants until it is almost entirely covered. Bake in a preheated oven at gas mark 5, 190°C (375°F) for 30 minutes. Serve hot with cream.

CHILLED REDCURRANT SOUFFLÉ

Serves 8

450g, 1lb redcurrants
5 eggs, separated
75g 3oz caster sugar
1 sachet of gelatine
juice of 1 lemon
150ml, ¼pt double cream, whipped

Gently heat the redcurrants and simmer until the juices run, then purée and sieve them. Whisk the egg yolks and sugar until pale and thick. Whisk in the redcurrant purée. Dissolve the gelatine in the lemon juice over a gentle heat and whisk into the egg yolk mixture. Fold in the cream and lastly whisk the egg whites and fold them in too. Chill until set.

ICED REDCURRANT MERINGUE

Serves 6 – 8

350g, 12oz redcurrants
50g, 2oz icing sugar
3 tbsp lemon juice
300ml, ½pt double cream
150ml, ¼pt single cream
8 meringues
225g, 8oz raspberries

Mix the redcurrants with the icing sugar and lemon juice. Purée and sieve them. Whip the creams together. Break up the meringues and mix with the cream. Stir the redcurrant purée into the meringue mixture to give a marbled effect. Pour into a ring mould and freeze for about 6 hours. Remove from the freezer and turn out. Pile the raspberries in the centre of the ring and serve.

REDCURRANT AND HONEY ICE CREAM

Serves 6 – 8

450g, 1lb redcurrants
3 tbsp clear honey
3 egg yolks
75g, 3oz granulated sugar
120ml, 4 fl oz water
300ml, ½pt whipping cream

Purée the redcurrants and sieve them. Mix the honey into the redcurrant purée. Meanwhile dissolve the sugar in the water and boil for 5 minutes. Beat the egg yolks until thick. Pour the sugar syrup onto the egg yolks while continuing to whisk until you have a frothy, creamy mixture. Whip the cream and fold into the egg mixture along with the redcurrant purée. When everything is evenly blended pour into a freezer container and freeze for an hour. Take out and beat the mixture to help reduce ice crystals and beat again after another hour. Return to the freezer and freeze until firm.

REDCURRANT JELLY

Redcurrants are naturally rich in pectin and acid so do not need a preserving sugar but need a higher proportion of sugar and more water can be used than with other fruits to produce a higher yield.

Makes about 1.5kg (3lb)

1kg, 2lb 2oz redcurrants
900ml, 1½pt water
750g, 1½lb sugar

Put the redcurrants in a saucepan with the water and heat slowly. Simmer until the redcurrants are soft. Mash them with a wooden spoon and strain through muslin. Put the juice in a large saucepan with the sugar. Heat gently, stirring until the sugar has dissolved, then boil rapidly until setting point is reached. Pour into small jars and seal.

REDCURRANT AND APPLE JELLY

This jelly goes well with lamb.

Makes about 4½kg (10lb)

900g, 2lb redcurrants
1.4kg, 3lb cooking apples, cored and chopped
1 litre, 1¾pt water
granulated sugar

Put the redcurrants and apples in a large saucepan or preserving pan and add the water. Bring to the boil and then simmer for about 1 hour. Beat well and put the mixture through a sieve. Measure the juice and add 450g (1lb) of sugar per 600ml (1pt) of juice. Heat until the sugar dissolves and then boil rapidly until setting point is reached. Pour into warmed jars and seal.

BLUEBERRIES

Blueberries, prevalent in America, have become more popular here in recent years. They are a good source of Vitamin C, iron and fibre and 100g of fruit = 60 calories. They freeze well and are a versatile berry which can be used in sauces to accompany meat as well as in many puddings either on their own or combined with other fruit.

SAVOURY RECIPES

SWEET RECIPES

BLUEBERRY AND BACON SALAD

Serves 2 –3

100g, 4oz streaky bacon, fried until crisp
100g, 4oz endive and radicchio salad leaves
2 tbsp pecan nuts, chopped

Dressing

4 tbsp olive oil
2 tbsp balsamic vinegar
100g, 4oz blueberries
salt and pepper

parmesan cheese shavings

Chop the bacon into small pieces and arrange in a salad bowl with the salad leaves and pecan nuts. To make the dressing, heat the olive oil and vinegar gently in a pan and add the blueberries. Season with salt and pepper and heat until just about to boil and then pour this hot dressing over the salad. Serve with shavings of parmesan cheese.

CHILLED BLUEBERRY SOUP

Serves 4

350ml, 12fl oz cranberry juice
240ml, 8fl oz red wine
1 cinnamon stick
100g, 4oz caster sugar
225g, 8oz blueberries
1 tbsp cornflour blended with 2 tbsp water
210ml, 7fl oz crème fraîche

Put the cranberry juice, wine and cinnamon stick into a saucepan. Add the sugar and simmer for 15 minutes. Stir the blueberries into the liquid, reserving a few for decoration. Cook for 5 minutes. Gradually blend the cornflour into the soup and bring back to the boil. Cook for several more minutes until the soup thickens. Then remove the cinnamon stick and cool the soup. Stir in the crème fraîche, cover and chill for several hours. Decorate with the reserved blueberries before serving.

PHEASANT WITH BLUEBERRIES

Serves 4

4 pheasant breasts with skin
2 tbsp olive oil
90ml, 3fl oz red wine
180ml, 6fl oz crème fraîche
2 tbsp crème de cassis
150g, 6oz blueberries

Heat the oil in a frying pan and brown the breasts all over. Lower the heat and cook for about 10 minutes turning half way through. Then turn up the heat and add the red wine. Let it bubble away and reduce a little. Then stir in the crème fraîche and cassis. Cook for a few minutes until thickened. Stir in the blueberries and gently heat through. Serve with rice or pasta and a salad.

BLUEBERRY AND NECTARINE COBBLER

This is a family pudding and is quite filling.

Serves 6

6 nectarines, stoned and sliced
225g, 8oz blueberries
50g, 2oz light muscovado sugar

For the cobbler

225g, 8oz self-raising flour
75g, 3oz butter
50g, 2oz light muscovado sugar
grated rind of 1 lemon
150ml, ¼pt natural yoghurt

Put the nectarine slices and blueberries in an ovenproof dish and sprinkle over the sugar. To make the cobbler, rub the butter into the flour, stir in the sugar and grated lemon. Make a well in the centre and add the yoghurt. Mix the yoghurt in gradually until everything is well combined. Spoon over the fruit and bake in a preheated oven at gas mark 6, 200°C (400°F) for 20 minutes. The filling will bubble through the cobbler. Serve hot with single cream.

APPLE AND BLUEBERRY WALNUT CRISP

The blueberries give the inside of this pudding great colour. The apples melt into the purple fruit.

Serves 4 - 6

350g, 12oz blueberries
225g, 8oz cooking apples, peeled, cored and sliced
juice and grated rind of 1 lemon
150g, 6oz light brown sugar

For the topping

150g, 6oz plain flour
100g, 4oz granulated sugar
1 tsp baking powder
50g, 2oz butter
1 large egg, beaten
a handful of walnuts, chopped
½ tsp cinnamon

Mix the blueberries and apples with the lemon rind, juice and the brown sugar and put in a greased ovenproof dish. To make the topping, mix together the flour, baking powder and sugar. Rub in the butter, then add the egg and nuts. Spread this mixture over the fruit. Sprinkle the cinnamon over the top. Cook in a preheated oven at gas mark 6, 200°C (400°F) for 30 minutes. The top should be nicely browned. Serve with cream or crème fraîche.

PINEAPPLE AND BLUEBERRY
UPSIDE DOWN PUDDING

Serves 6 - 8

For the base

50g, 2oz butter
50g, 2oz brown sugar
75g, 3oz blueberries
small can of pineapple chunks

For the sponge

100g, 4oz caster sugar
100g, 4oz butter
2 eggs
150g, 6oz self-raising flour
2 tbsp milk

Grease a 20cm (8in) deep cake tin. Cream together the butter and brown sugar and spread over the base of the tin. Arrange the pineapple chunks and blueberries over the top. Beat together all the ingredients for the sponge, adding the milk to give the mixture a dropping consistency. Then spread over the top of the pineapple and blueberries. Bake in the oven at gas mark 4, 180°C (350°F) for about 45 minutes. Turn out and serve with cream.

BLUEBERRY PIE

Serves 4 - 6

450g, 1lb blueberries
75g, 3oz caster sugar
3 tbsp cornflour
grated rind and juice of half an orange
grated rind of half a lemon
½ tsp cinnamon

150g, 6oz shortcrust pastry
beaten egg to glaze
Sprinkling of caster sugar

Mix the cornflour, sugar, orange juice and orange and lemon rinds into the blueberries and sprinkle on the cinnamon. Transfer to a pie dish. Roll out the pastry to form a lid and cover the blueberries. Glaze with the beaten egg and sprinkle with caster sugar. Bake in the oven at gas mark 4, 180°C (350°F) for 30 minutes and serve hot with cream.

BLUEBERRY AND LEMON CHEESECAKE

Serves 6 - 8

150g, 6oz sweet pastry (see page 38)

Filling

100g, 4oz butter
100g, 4oz caster sugar
3 eggs, beaten
1 tbsp plain flour
grated peel and juice of 2 small lemons
1 tsp vanilla essence
450g, 1lb cream cheese
2 tbsp milk

Topping

350g, 12oz blueberries
150ml, ¼pt double cream

Roll out the pastry and line a greased 20cm (8in) springform cake tin. Chill while you make the filling. Cream the butter and sugar together and gradually add the eggs and the flour. Beat in the lemon peel, juice and vanilla essence. In another bowl beat the cream cheese and milk and then add to the butter mixture and beat well together. Pour this into the chilled pastry case and bake at gas mark 3, 160°C (325°F) for about an hour or until set and golden on top. Turn the oven off and allow to cool gradually in the oven – this will help stop any cracks appearing. Turn out of the tin, whip the cream and spread over the cheesecake when cool. Arrange the blueberries over the cream and serve.

BLUEBERRY FRANGIPANE TART

Serves 8

For the base

150g, 6oz plain flour
100g, 4oz caster sugar
100g, 4oz butter

For the filling

200g, 7oz butter
200g, 7oz caster sugar
1 egg and 2 egg yolks
6 tbsp plain flour, sieved
150g, 6oz ground almonds
4 tbsp double cream
225g, 8oz blueberries

To make the base, place the flour and sugar in a bowl and rub in the butter. Add a tablespoon of water and knead together until you have a soft dough. Chill for 30 minutes. Roll out the dough and line a greased 23cm (9in) flan tin. Prick the pastry and bake in a preheated oven at gas mark 5, 190°C (375°F) for 15 minutes. To make the filling, cream together the butter and sugar. Beat in the egg and egg yolks and stir in the flour, almonds and cream. Spread the blueberries over the base of the pastry and spoon the filling on top. Bake in the oven at gas mark 4, 180°C (350°F) for about 45 minutes or until the topping has set.

BLUEBERRY CUSTARD TART

Serves 6 - 8

For the base

225g, 8oz digestive biscuits, crushed
75g, 3oz butter, melted

Filling

600ml, 1pt milk
4 egg yolks
50g, 2oz sugar
1 tsp cornflour
50g, 2oz ground almonds
2 egg whites, whisked
350g, 12oz blueberries

Mix the biscuit crumbs and melted butter together and use to line a 20cm (8in) flan dish. Whisk the egg yolks, sugar and cornflour together briefly. Warm the milk and pour onto the egg yolk mixture. Mix well and cook over a low heat, stirring constantly until the mixture thickens. Fold in the almonds and whisked egg whites. Lay the blueberries over the biscuit base and pour the custard mixture on top. Bake in the oven at gas mark 5, 190°C (375°F) for about 30 minutes until the custard has set. Eat warm with cream or cold.

BLUEBERRY AND PEAR CRUMBLE

Serves 4

100g, 4oz blueberries
450g, 1lb fresh pears, peeled, cored and sliced

Crumble

75g, 3oz plain flour
75g, 3oz soft brown sugar
50g, 2oz porridge oats
½ tsp cinnamon
75g, 3oz butter

Put the sliced pears in an ovenproof dish and add the blueberries. Mix the flour, brown sugar, oats and cinnamon together. Then rub in the butter. Spread this mixture over the fruit. Bake in a preheated oven at gas mark 5, 190°C (375°F) for about 30 minutes. Serve with cream.

BLUEBERRY CHARLOTTE

Serves 4 - 6

350g, 12oz blueberries
75g, 3oz butter, melted
100g, 4oz caster sugar
3 eating apples, cored, peeled and sliced
180ml, 6fl oz apple juice
200g, 7oz white bread, cut into cubes

Brush a round 23cm (9in) ovenproof dish with some of the melted butter and dust with caster sugar. Mix together the blueberries, apples, apple juice, bread cubes and the rest of the sugar and butter. Spoon the mixture into the dish and spread it out evenly. Place on a baking tray and bake uncovered in the oven at gas mark 5, 190°C (375°F) for 30 minutes until crisp and golden. Leave to cool for a few minutes before turning out and serve with crème fraîche.

PANCAKE STREUDELS WITH BLUEBERRIES

Serves 8

8 pancakes
75g, 3oz butter
75g, 3oz brown sugar
3 eating apples, peeled, cored and diced
225g, 8oz blueberries
75g, 3oz pecans
2 tsp lemon juice

Heat the butter and sugar in a frying pan. Toss in the diced apples and fry for a few minutes until softened. Add the blueberries and the pecans and fry for a couple more minutes. Add the lemon juice. Spoon some of the filling into each pancake. Fold the sides over to enclose the filling and turn over. Sprinkle with icing sugar and serve.

BLUEBERRY AND VANILLA PAVLOVA

Serves 6 - 8

For the pavlova

4 egg whites
225g, 8oz caster sugar
1 tsp vanilla essence
1 tsp cornflour
1 tsp white wine vinegar
pinch of cream of tartar

Topping

225g, 8oz blueberries
25g, 1oz caster sugar
225g, 8oz mascarpone
2 tbsp light muscovado sugar
150ml, ¼pt Greek yoghurt
1 tbsp lemon juice

To make the pavlova whisk the egg whites and continue whisking them while gradually adding the caster sugar. Fold in the vanilla essence, vinegar, cornflour and cream of tartar. Spread the mixture in a circle on a greased baking sheet and bake in a preheated oven at gas mark 4, 180°C (350°F) for 5 minutes then reduce to gas mark 1, 120°C (275°F) and cook for an hour. Then transfer to a serving plate. Put the blueberries in a small saucepan with the sugar. Heat gently until the sugar dissolves and the blueberries soften. Leave to cool. Beat the mascarpone and stir in the sugar, yoghurt and lemon juice. Spread the mascarpone mixture over the pavlova and cover with the blueberries.

BLUEBERRY ICE CREAM

Serves 4

2 eggs, separated
3 tbsp blackcurrant juice such as Ribena
75g, 3oz caster sugar
300ml, ½pt double cream, whipped
225g, 8oz blueberries

Whisk the egg yolks and sugar until pale and thick and then add the blackcurrant juice and whisk again. Whisk the egg whites. Fold the cream into the egg yolk mixture, then the egg whites and finally fold in the blueberries. Spoon into a freezer container and freeze. Remove from the freezer about 20 minutes before serving.

BLUEBERRY AND ALMOND MUFFINS

Makes 12

125g, 5oz plain flour
2 tsp baking powder
½ tsp cinnamon
100g, 4oz granulated sugar
1 large egg
50g, 2oz melted butter
150ml, ¼pt milk
1 tsp grated lemon zest
½ tsp almond essence
125g, 5oz blueberries
125g, 5oz almonds, toasted and chopped

Sift the flour, baking power and cinnamon. Whisk the sugar and egg together and then beat in the melted butter, milk, lemon zest and almond essence. Stir this liquid mixture into the dry ingredients. Fold in the blueberries and nuts. Divide the mixture between 12 greased muffin cases. Bake in a preheated oven at gas mark 6, 200°C (400°F) for 20 minutes.

CHERRIES

Cherries come in many varieties and can be divided into three groups: sweet, sour, and hybrid cherries. The sour cherries are chiefly morellos and of the hybrid cherries a popular one is Duke. They contain Vitamin A and C and some fibre. Calories vary depending on the type – sour cherries would give about 56 calories per 100g and sweet ones upto 77 calories per 100g.

SAVOURY RECIPES

SWEET RECIPES

CHERRY AND WALNUT SALAD

Serves 4

350g, 12oz black cherries, halved and stoned
50g, 2oz walnut pieces
1 orange
mixed salad leaves, such as rocket, endive, radicchio
and lamb's lettuce

Dressing

3tbsp olive oil
1 tbsp lemon juice
pinch of dry mustard
salt and pepper

Peel the orange and slice thinly. Arrange the salad leaves on a serving dish and add the orange slices. Then scatter the halved cherries and walnuts over the top. To make the dressing, mix together the olive oil, lemon juice, mustard and seasoning and pour over the salad.

CHICKEN SALAD WITH TARRAGON AND CHERRIES

Serves 8

Meat from 1 large cooked chicken
2 eggs
4 tbsp caster sugar
6 tbsp white wine vinegar
1 tbsp chopped fresh tarragon
150ml, ¼pt double cream
450g, 1lb cherries, halved and stoned
chopped chives

Beat the eggs and caster sugar together until they are thick and pale. Continue whisking while you gradually add the vinegar. Whip the cream and fold it in to the egg and vinegar mixture along with the chopped tarragon. Fold in the chopped cherries. Slice the cooked chicken and arrange on a serving plate. Spread the cherry and cream mixture all over the chicken and garnish with chopped chives.

CHERRY COMPOTE

Serves 4 – 6

450g, 1lb cherries, stoned
50g, 2oz caster sugar
1 tbsp redcurrant jelly
150ml, ¼pt red wine
grated rind and juice of 1 orange

Melt the redcurrant jelly in a frying pan with the sugar. Add the cherries and cook for a few minutes until the juices run. Pour in the wine, orange juice and add the grated rind. Simmer for a couple of minutes. Serve hot or cold.

CHERRY SOUFFLÉ OMELETTE

Serves 4

225g, 8oz black cherries, stoned
2 tbsp brandy
4 eggs, separated
2 tsp flour
1 tbsp icing sugar
15g, ½oz butter
icing sugar for sprinkling

Marinade the cherries in the brandy and icing sugar for about an hour. Whisk the egg yolks together until light and creamy and whisk the egg whites until stiff. Fold the whites and flour into the egg yolks. Heat the butter in a frying pan and pour in half the egg mixture. Scatter the cherries on top and cover with the remaining egg. Cook for a couple of minutes and then finish off under the grill. Sprinkle with some icing sugar and serve at once.

CHERRY AND ALMOND TART

Serves 6

225g, 8oz shortcrust pastry
50g, 2oz digestive biscuits, crushed
450g, 1lb black cherries, halved and stoned
50g, 2oz butter
50g, 2oz sugar
1 egg
25g, 1oz plain flour
75g, 3oz ground almonds

Roll out two thirds of the pastry and line a greased 20cm (8in) flan dish. Sprinkle the biscuit crumbs over the pastry. Lay the cherries over the crumbs. Cream the butter and sugar, beat in the egg and add the flour and ground almonds. Spread this mixture evenly over the cherries. Use the remaining pastry to make a lattice design over the tart. Brush with milk and bake in a preheated oven at gas mark 6, 200°C (400°F) for about 40 minutes.

CHERRY AND REDCURRANT
UPSIDE DOWN CAKE

Serves 6

225g, 8oz cherries, halved and stoned
100g, 4oz redcurrants
75g, 3oz caster sugar
75g, 3oz soft brown sugar
75g, 3oz butter
3 eggs
125g, 5oz self-raising flour, sieved
a few drops of vanilla essence

Arrange the cherries and redcurrants over the base of a greased 20cm (8in) cake tin. Sprinkle the caster sugar over them. Cream together the butter and brown sugar and gradually add the eggs alternately with the flour. Beat in the vanilla essence. Pour the mixture over the fruit and smooth the top. Bake in the oven at gas mark 4, 180°C (350°F) for 30 minutes or until a skewer stuck in the middle comes out clean. Invert the pudding onto a plate and serve with cream.

CHERRY CLAFOUTIS

Serves 4 – 6

75g, 3oz flour
3 eggs
300ml, ½pt milk
350g, 12oz black cherries, stoned
50g, 2oz brown sugar

Sift the flour into a bowl, make a well in the centre and drop in the eggs. Beat and then add the milk and mix until smooth. Leave to stand for 30 minutes. In a baking tin heat a spoonful of oil until it is really hot. Pour in the batter mixture and lay the cherries on top. Sprinkle with the brown sugar and put in a preheated oven at gas mark 7, 220°C (425°F) for about 20 minutes and then lower the heat to gas mark 5, 190°C (375°F) and cook for another 10 minutes. Serve warm with extra sugar if necessary and cream.

CHERRY ICE CREAM

Serves 6

300ml, ½pt milk
3 egg yolks
125g, 5oz sugar
150ml, ¼pt single cream
150ml, ¼pt crème fraîche
450g, 1lb cherries, stoned and halved

Heat the milk in a saucepan until just below boiling point. Put the egg yolks and sugar in a bowl and whisk together until pale and thick and then whisk in the hot milk. Return to the saucepan and cook over a low heat, stirring all the time until the custard thickens. Cool and stir in the single cream and crème fraîche. Pour into a freezer container, cover and freeze for an hour, then take out and beat to help reduce ice crystals. Beat again after another hour and fold in the cherries. Freeze again until firm.

GOOSEBERRIES

Gooseberries, native to Europe and North America, grew wild all over Britain for centuries before being cultivated in the 1500s. They are high in Vitamin C and also contain vitamins A and D, potassium, calcium, phosphorus and niacin. They are very low in calories - 100g = 17 calories. Being rich in pectin, gooseberries make excellent jam. They have a long season – early green gooseberries can be cooked and used in fruit fools, pies etc. There are many varieties of gooseberries which range in colour from bright green to a wonderful purple.

SAVOURY RECIPES

SWEET RECIPES

MACKEREL WITH GOOSEBERRY SAUCE

Serves 4

4 mackerel, filleted
2 tbsp fine oatmeal
salt and pepper
knob of butter
225g, 8oz gooseberries
1 tsp brown sugar
1 egg, beaten

Season the mackerel inside and out with salt and pepper. Sprinkle the oatmeal evenly over the mackerel and dot with butter. Cook under a preheated grill for 20 minutes. Meanwhile make the sauce. Sieve the gooseberries to remove the pips. Put the purée in a small saucepan with the sugar and beat in the egg, warming gently and stirring. Place the mackerel on a warm serving dish and spoon over the sauce.

HERRINGS WITH GOOSEBERRY SAUCE

Serves 4

4 herrings, gutted and with heads removed
225g, 8oz gooseberries
25g, 1oz sugar
pinch of ground ginger

Grill the herrings for 5 minutes on each side. Meanwhile make a sauce by cooking the gooseberries in a covered saucepan over a gentle heat until the juices run. Purée and add the sugar and ginger. Serve with the herrings.

BACON CHOPS WITH GOOSEBERRIES

This dish could be served with mashed potato and red cabbage.

Serves 4

1 tbsp soft brown sugar
1 tsp mustard powder
4 bacon chops
15g, ½oz butter
1 onion, skinned and chopped
150ml, ¼pt vegetable stock
100g, 4oz gooseberries

Mix together the brown sugar and mustard and rub into the bacon chops. Fry the onion in the butter in a large frying pan. Add the bacon chops, half the stock and the gooseberries. Simmer gently for 15 minutes. Remove the chops. Purée and sieve the gooseberry and onion mixture so that you have a smooth sauce. Return the chops and purée to the pan and add the rest of the stock. Simmer for another 10 minutes.

CHILLED GOOSEBERRY CHEESECAKE

Serves 8

150g, 6oz digestive biscuits, crushed
75g, 3oz butter
225g, 8oz gooseberries
100g, 4oz caster sugar
1 tbsp water
350g, 12oz cream cheese
2 eggs, separated
1 sachet gelatine
300ml, ½pt double cream

Melt the butter and stir into the biscuit crumbs. Use this biscuit mixture to line the base of a greased 20cm (8in) tin. Cook the gooseberries in a pan with the water and sugar until soft. Then purée and sieve them to remove the pips. Mix together the cream cheese and egg yolks and stir in the gooseberry purée. Whip the cream and fold it in. Dissolve the gelatine in a little water and stir into the mixture. Whisk the egg whites until stiff and fold them in. Pour the cheesecake mixture onto the biscuit base and transfer to the fridge to set.

GOOSEBERRY AND ELDERFLOWER FOOL

Serves 4 - 6

450g, 1lb gooseberries
2 tbsp water
2 heads of elderflowers
100g, 4oz caster sugar
1 egg white
300ml, ½pt double cream

Place the gooseberries in a saucepan with the water and elderflowers. Bring to the boil and simmer for about 10 minutes until soft. Then stir in the sugar. Sieve the fruit and allow the purée to cool. Whip up the cream and egg white in separate bowls and fold them both into the gooseberry purée. Chill before serving.

GOOSEBERRY MERINGUE

Serves 4 – 6

450g, 1lb gooseberries, topped and tailed
2 tbsp honey
2 egg whites
75g, 3oz light soft brown sugar

Put the gooseberries in a pan with a tablespoon of water. Cook gently until soft and add the honey. Spoon into an ovenproof dish. Whisk the egg whites until stiff and then whisk in half the sugar. Fold in the remaining sugar with a metal spoon and spread over the gooseberries. Place in a preheated oven at gas mark 4, 180°C (350°F) for 20 minutes or until the meringue is just turning brown on top. Serve warm or cold with cream.

GOOSEBERRY AND ORANGE JAM

Makes about 3kg (6½lb)

1.8kg, 4lb gooseberries, topped and tailed
8 tbsp grated orange rind
12 tbsp orange juice
450ml, ¾pt water
1.8kg, 4lb preserving sugar

Place the gooseberries in a large pan. Add the orange rind, juice and water. Bring to the boil and simmer until the gooseberries are soft. Add the sugar. Heat gently, stirring until the sugar has dissolved. Bring to the boil, then boil rapidly until setting point is reached. Remove the scum. Cool slightly and then pour into warmed jars and seal.

GOOSEBERRY AND RHUBARB JAM

Makes 1.8kg (4lb)

675g, 1½lb rhubarb, cut into chunks
675g, 1½lb gooseberries, topped and tailed
1.4kg, 3lb granulated sugar
300ml, ½pt water
juice of 1 lemon
knob of butter

Put the rhubarb, gooseberries, sugar, lemon juice and water in a large saucepan. Simmer for 30 minutes until soft. Bring to the boil and boil rapidly for 20 minutes. Test for a set. Remove from the heat and add the butter which will remove any scum. Pour into warmed jars and seal.

GOOSEBERRY CHUTNEY

Makes about 2.25kg (5lb)

1.4kg, 3lb gooseberries, topped and tailed
225g, 8oz raisins
350g, 12oz onions, peeled and chopped
15g, ½oz mustard seed, crushed
½ tsp cayenne pepper
¼ tsp ground mace
1 tbsp salt
900g, 2lb muscovado sugar
900ml, 1½pt malt vinegar

Put all the ingredients into a pan and bring slowly to simmering point. Cook over a low heat until the fruit is blended with the other ingredients and the vinegar has been absorbed. This will take about 2 hours. Stir with a wooden spoon and pour into warmed jars. Seal and store.

MIXED FRUIT RECIPES

QUICK SUMMER PUDDING

Serves 6

900g, 2lb mixed fruits such as strawberries, raspberries,
black and redcurrants
150g, 6oz golden caster sugar
8-10 slices of white bread, crusts removed

Put the sugar and 90ml (3fl oz) of water in a pan with the
red and blackcurrants and heat to dissolve the sugar. Then
add the raspberries and strawberries. Set aside for 10 minutes. Drain the juices from the fruit and dip each piece of
bread in the fruit juice. Then use the slices to line a 1.2
litre (2 pint) basin by overlapping the bread around the
sides. Don't cover the bottom with bread. Spoon the cooked
fruits into the basin. Spoon some of the juice over the
fruits. Press the remaining slices of bread over the fruit.
Loosen the sides and invert the pudding onto a plate. Spoon
over any remaining juices and serve straightaway with
cream.

TRADITIONAL SUMMER PUDDING

Serves 6

900g, 2lb summer fruits such as black and redcurrants,
raspberries, strawberries
150g, 6oz caster sugar
8 – 10 slices wholemeal bread, crusts removed

Cook the black and redcurrants adding 2 tablespoons of water and the sugar. After a few minutes add the raspberries and cook for a couple more minutes. Lastly add the strawberries and turn off the heat. Use the slices of bread to line a 1.2 litre (2 pint) basin including the bottom. Pour the cooked fruit into the bowl with all the juices. Press a slice of bread down on top and put a plate on top with a weight. Refrigerate overnight and when ready to serve, run a knife around the sides and turn the pudding out. Serve with cream or crème fraîche.

SUMMER PUDDING WITH NECTARINES

Serves 6

1 brioche loaf, sliced with crusts removed
6 large nectarines
450g, 1lb blackcurrants
225g, 8oz whitecurrants
150g, 6oz caster sugar

Use the brioche slices to line a 1.2 litre (2 pint) pudding basin. Put the black and whitecurrants in a saucepan with the sugar and cook gently until the juices run. Peel and dice the nectarines and add to the currants. Simmer for a few more minutes and then pour onto the brioche slices. Reserve any left over fruit and juice. Top with brioche slices to enclose the fruit. Cover with a plate and put a weight on top. Chill overnight. When you are ready to serve it turn the pudding out and cover any brioche slices not coloured with juice with the remaining fruit and juice.

SUMMER FRUITS CREAM

Serves 6

150g, 6oz raspberries
150g, 6oz strawberries
100g, 4oz blackcurrants
300ml, ½pt sweet cider
2 tbsp cornflour
150g, 6oz caster sugar
150ml, ¼pt double cream
2 tbsp Greek yoghurt

Sieve all the fruits and mix together. Add the cider. Blend the cornflour with 2 tablespoons of water and stir into the fruit purée and sugar. Pour the mixture into a saucepan and bring slowly to the boil, stirring. Cook for a minute. Cool and chill in a serving bowl or 6 individual dishes. Whip the cream and Greek yoghurt together and stir into the fruit purées to give a marbled effect. Serve straightaway.

RED BERRY JELLY

Serves 8

1½ sachets gelatine
225g, 8oz caster sugar
300ml, ½pt water
350g, 12oz raspberries
350g, 12 oz strawberries, sliced
350g, 12oz redcurrants
3 tbsp cassis

Sprinkle the gelatine over 4 tablespoons of the water. Meanwhile mix the sugar and the rest of the water in a saucepan and bring to the boil, stirring until the sugar dissolves. Simmer for 5 minutes then add all the fruit and bring back to the boil. Remove from the heat and add the cassis. Warm the gelatine until it dissolves and stir into the hot fruit. Divide the mixture between ramekin dishes or spoon into a serving bowl. Leave to set.

SOME ICE CREAMS WITH SUMMER FRUIT SAUCES

MASCARPONE ICE CREAM WITH BLACKCURRANT AND CHESTNUT SAUCE

Serves 6

For the ice cream

2 egg yolks
50g, 2oz icing sugar
225g, 8oz mascarpone
2 tsp vanilla essence

Whisk together the egg yolks and icing sugar until really thick. Beat the mascarpone and vanilla essence into the egg yolk mixture. Transfer to a freezer container and freeze until firm.

For the sauce

225g, 8oz blackcurrants, puréed and sieved
100g, 4oz sweetened chestnut purée (or unsweetened –
add 50g, 2oz brown sugar)

Mix the chestnut purée and blackcurrant juice together and serve with the ice cream.

WHITE CHOCOLATE ICE CREAM WITH STRAWBERRY SAUCE

Serves 8

For the ice cream

4 egg yolks
50g, 2oz caster sugar
250ml, 9fl oz milk
225g, 8oz white chocolate
250ml, 9fl oz cream, whipped

Put the egg yolks and sugar in a bowl and whisk until thick. Pour the milk into a saucepan and heat until it is nearly boiling. Remove from the heat and whisk into the egg yolks. Return to the pan and cook, stirring over a low heat until the mixture thickens. Put the chocolate in a bowl over a pan of simmering water and stir in the custard. When the chocolate has melted, stir the mixture and leave to cool. Fold in the whipped cream, pour into a freezer container and freeze until firm.

For the sauce

150g, 6oz strawberries
juice of 1 small orange
1 tbsp caster sugar

Whizz the strawberries with the orange juice and caster sugar in a processor and serve with the ice cream.

CINNAMON ICE CREAM WITH MIXED FRUIT SAUCE

Serves 8

For the ice cream

150ml, ¼pt milk
1 cinnamon stick
4 eggs, separated
25g, 1oz icing sugar, sifted
2 tsp cinnamon
100g, 4oz clear honey
150ml, ¼pt soured cream
125g, 5oz cream cheese

Heat the milk with the cinnamon stick to just below boiling point, and then cover and leave to infuse. Beat the egg yolks with the icing sugar and ground cinnamon. Remove the cinnamon stick and stir the honey into the milk. Heat to just below boiling point again and pour onto the egg yolks, whisking together. Beat the soured cream and cream cheese together and whisk into the egg yolk mixture. Finally whisk the egg whites and fold them in carefully. Transfer to a freezer container and freeze until firm.

For the sauce

225g, 8oz mixed black and redcurrants and raspberries
100g, 4oz caster sugar
1 tbsp cassis

Cook the blackcurrants and redcurrants with the sugar over a gentle heat until the juices begin to run. Add the raspberries and cook for a couple more minutes. Sieve this mixture, add the cassis and serve warm with the cinnamon ice cream.

SAFFRON ICE CREAM WITH BLUEBERRY SAUCE

Serves 4

For the ice cream

4 egg yolks
50g, 2oz caster sugar
300ml, ½pt milk
1 tsp saffron strands
60ml, 2fl oz cream, whipped

Whisk the egg yolks with the sugar until pale and thick. Heat the milk until nearly boiling and then whisk into the egg yolks. Return to the pan and cook, stirring all the time, until the mixture thickens. Remove from the heat and stir in the saffron. Leave to cool, stirring occasionally. Pour into a freezer container and freeze until just becoming firm. Beat well and fold in the cream. Freeze until firm.

For the sauce

225g, 8oz blueberries
1 tbsp caster sugar
1 tbsp finely chopped mint

Place the blueberries in a saucepan with the sugar and a tablespoon of water and cook for about 5 minutes. Remove half the blueberries and sieve them. Stir in the rest of the blueberries with the mint and leave to cool.

LEMON CURD ICE CREAM WITH RASPBERRY COULIS

Serves 6 – 8

For the ice cream

4 eggs, separated
225g, 8oz lemon curd
300ml, ½pt cream, whipped
50g, 2oz icing sugar

Whisk the egg yolks into the lemon curd. Fold in the whipped cream. Whisk the egg whites until becoming stiff and whisk in the icing sugar. Fold into the lemon curd mixture and stir until evenly incorporated. Transfer to a freezer container and freeze until firm.

For the sauce

225g, 8oz raspberries
50g, 2oz icing sugar
2 tbsp lemon juice

Put the raspberries in a saucepan with the lemon juice and caster sugar. Heat gently for about 5 minutes and then sieve them. Serve with the ice cream.

CHOCOLATE ICE CREAM WITH CHERRY SAUCE

Serves 6

For the ice cream

100g, 4oz dark chocolate
1 small tin of condensed milk
300ml, ½pt double cream, lightly whipped
½ tsp vanilla essence

Dissolve the chocolate in the condensed milk in a bowl over a pan of simmering water. Remove from the heat and stir in the vanilla essence and 4 tablespoons of water. Leave to cool. Fold in the whipped cream, pour into a freezer container and freeze until firm.

For the sauce

450g, 1lb cherries, halved and stoned
3 tbsp sugar
150ml, ¼pt water
3 tbsp Kirsch

Put the cherries in a saucepan with the sugar and water. Simmer for about 5 minutes until the juices run, then turn up the heat and boil until the juice reduces and becomes syrupy. Remove from the heat and cool. Stir in the Kirsch. Serve with the ice cream.

PEACH AND HAZELNUT ICE CREAM WITH RASPBERRY AND REDCURRANT SAUCE

Serves 4

For the ice cream

4 peaches
4 tbsp honey
3 egg yolks
150ml, ¼pt double cream, whipped
50g, 2oz chopped hazelnuts
few drops of lemon juice

Peel the peaches, remove the stones and purée the flesh. Put the honey and 1 tablespoon of water in a saucepan and heat gently to melt the honey. Then bring to boiling point. Whisk the egg yolks and pour the hot syrup in a steady stream on to the egg yolks whisking all the time. Over a pan of simmering water continue to whisk until the mixture thickens. Whisk the peach purée and hazelnuts into the egg yolk mixture. Fold in the cream and add a little lemon juice. Pour into a freezer container and freeze until firm.

For the sauce

75g, 3oz redcurrants
50g, 2oz caster sugar
75g, 3oz raspberries

Heat the redcurrants with the sugar until the juices run. Add the raspberries. Purée and sieve the mixture and serve warm or cold with the ice cream.

ZABAGLIONE ICE CREAM WITH RASPBERRY AND BLACKCURRANT SAUCE

Serves 6 – 8

For the ice cream

4 egg yolks
75g, 3oz caster sugar
120ml, 4fl oz Marsala
300ml, ½pt double cream

Put the egg yolks and sugar in a bowl and beat over a saucepan of simmering water until very pale and thick. Then gradually add the Marsala, a tablespoon at a time while you continue to whisk. You will need to whisk for about 20 minutes. You must add the Marsala slowly and allow the mixture to thicken or it will separate. Whip the double cream until fairly thick and gently fold into the egg mixture. Pour into a freezer container and freeze until firm.

For the sauce

100g, 4oz blackcurrants
100g, 4oz raspberries
75g, 3oz sugar
1 tbsp cassis

Gently heat the blackcurrants with the sugar until the juices begin to run. Add the raspberries and cook for a couple more minutes. Then purée and sieve the fruit. Stir in the cassis. Serve warm or cold with the ice cream.